Naturalizing the Mind

The Jean Nicod Lectures
François Recanati, editor

The Elm and the Expert: Mentalese and Its Semantics,
Jerry A. Fodor (1994)

Naturalizing the Mind, Fred Dretske (1995)

The 1994 Jean Nicod
Lectures

Naturalizing the Mind

Fred Dretske

A Bradford Book
The MIT Press
Cambridge, Massachusetts
London, England

© 1995 Massachusetts Institute of Technology
All rights reserved. No part of this book may be reproduced in any form by
any electronic or mechanical means (including photocopying, recording, or
information storage and retrieval) without permission in writing from the
publisher.

CNRS Editions will distribute the English-language edition in France,
Belgium, and Switzerland.

This book was set in Palatino by The MIT Press and was printed and bound
in the United States of America.

Library of Congress Cataloging-in-Publication Data

Dretske, Fred I.
  Naturalizing the mind / Fred Dretske.
      p.   cm.—(The Jean Nicod lectures; 1995)
  Includes bibliographical references (p.   ) and index.
  ISBN 0-262-04149-9 (hc : alk. paper)
  1. Philosophy of mind. I. Title. II. Series.
BD418.3.D74 1995
128′.2—dc20
                                                                    95-2229
                                                                       CIP

Contents

Series Foreword

The Jean Nicod Lectures are delivered annually in Paris by a leading philosopher of mind or philosophically oriented cognitive scientist. The 1993 inaugural lectures marked the centenary of the birth of the French philosopher and logician Jean Nicod (1893–1931). The lectures are sponsored by the Centre National de la Recherche Scientifique (CNRS) as part of its effort to develop the interdisciplinary field of cognitive science in France. The series hosts the texts of the lectures or the monographs they inspire.

Jacues Bouveresse, President of the Jean Nicod Committee
André Holley, Secretary of the Cognitive Science Program, CNRS
François Recanati, Secretary of the Jean Nicod Committee and Editor of the Series

Jean Nicod Committee

Mario Borillo

Jean-Pierre Changeux

Claude Debru

Jean-Gabriel Ganascia

Michel Imbert

Pierre Jacob

Jacques Mehler

Philippe de Rouilhan

Dan Sperber

Acknowledgments

I am grateful to CNRS, The Centre National de la Recherche Scientifique of France, for inviting me to give these lectures in Paris in the spring of 1994 at the second annual Conférence Jean Nicod de Philosophie Cognitive. Without the stimulus that this conference provided—actually, the threat of embarrassing myself before a French audience— these ideas would probably never have been assembled in such a timely way. They might not have been assembled at all.

My weeks in Paris were made particularly memorable— both socially and philosophically—by a group of philosophers and scientists, faculty and students alike (most of them, I think, at CREA, Centre de Recherche en Epistémologie Appliquée), who were not only gracious hosts, but challenging critics after each lecture. It was a humbling experience to find myself arguing technical issues in the philosophy of mind with French philosophers—in the middle of Paris no less—*in English*. Imagine what they would have done to me in French. I particularly want to thank Pierre Jacob for everything he did—and there were many things—to make my visit so pleasant.

Thanks to the Stanford Humanities Center I was able to devote almost the full year to preparing these lectures. I was a fellow there during the year 1993–1994 and I am deeply grateful to the support I received from the director, Wanda Corn, the associate director, Charles Junkerman, and the fellows and staff. No one *ever* knocked on my door. They obviously know how to run a research institute.

I really started working on these lectures (without realizing it) in 1991 when I was preparing talks to give in Valencia, Spain. The Valencia lectures were early stabs at these topics—so early, in fact, that I did not want to publish the results. I wish to thank the philosophers in Spain, and especially Josep Corbi, for their hospitality and helpful discussion.

Students and friends read some—and in a few cases all—of these lectures and gave me useful comments and criticism. I want to thank Sven Bernecker, and Tim Schroeder here at Stanford, Murat Aydede now at Chicago, and Eric Schwitzgebel at Berkeley for their help. They made more of a difference than might be apparent to them. David Rosenthal read most of the lectures and provided useful comments—especially on chapter 4. Berent Enc, an old friend from Wisconsin, gave me months of grief by not letting me ignore problems I didn't know how to solve He made me start thinking about chapter 5 two years before I got around to writing it. Georges Rey not only read the manuscript—several times as far as I can tell—but gave me a truly astonishing number of useful suggestions and criticisms. Every author should be so fortunate. I am deeply grateful to him. I tried, as best I could, to respond to his criticisms in final revisions, but some of our differences went far too deep. To keep the book a reasonable approximation to the lectures I gave in Paris, I had to ignore many of

Georges's most perceptive and challenging questions. Sorry about that. We will, I'm sure, come back to them.

Finally, I would like to thank Güven Güzeldere. He arrived at Stanford a few years ago and promptly got me worrying about *his* problems. I thought it was supposed to go the other way around. No matter. We are now both worried about them. I thank him for making me realize, patiently and with great insight, how really hard these problems are.

Prologue

The purpose of these lectures is to promote a naturalistic theory of the mind—something I call the Representational Thesis. The thesis, in two parts, is that, plus or minus a bit,[1] (1) *All mental facts are representational facts*, and (2) *All representational facts are facts about informational functions*. The reason I am interested in this thesis is that, as far as I can tell, it is the only approach to the topic of consciousness that has much to say about the baffling problems of phenomenal experience. It does not, to be sure, remove *all* the mysteries. It removes enough of them, though, to justify putting one's money on the nose of this philosophical horse. That, at least, is where my money is. These lectures are an attempt to convince others that the smart money belongs there.

Representational Naturalism (as I shall call the view defined by the Representational Thesis) helps one understand, for example, why conscious experiences have that peculiar diaphanous quality—the quality of always being present *when*, but never *where*, one looks to find them. It provides a satisfying account of the qualitative, the first-person, aspect of our sensory and affective life—distinguishing, in naturalistic terms, between *what* we experience (reality) and *how* we experience it (appearance). In providing this account, it establishes a framework within which subjectivity can be studied objectively. It demystifies introspection: the mind's knowledge of itself no longer requires an internal "eye" observing the clockwork of the mind. And it provides an answer—a biologically plausible answer—to questions about the function or purpose of consciousness. These benefits, and more, derive from conceiving of the mind as the representational face of the brain.

A working premise behind the Representational Thesis is that a better understanding of *the mind* is not to be obtained by knowledge—no matter how detailed and precise—of the biological machinery by means of which the mind does its job. Information about the wetware may be useful, but it is not enough. If you don't know what a camera is, it is of no help to be told about *f*-stops, focal lengths, shutter speeds, and ASA numbers. What you need to know is something more basic, something about pictures, something about what cameras *do*. Without that you don't know what a camera is no matter how much you know about the machinery by means of which cameras do their job. Since the manipulation and use of representations is the primary job of the mind, a deeper understanding of the nature of representation and its naturalistic basis is, perforce, a deeper understanding of the mind.

The Representational Thesis is plausible enough for the propositional attitudes—belief, thought, judgment, and the like. I have given my own account of the propositional attitudes—particularly belief and desire—in Dretske (1988). The thesis is less plausible—some would say completely implausible—for sensory affairs, for the phenomenal or qualitative aspects of our mental life. Nonetheless, in these lectures I concentrate on perceptual experience. The topic is qualia—that dimension of our conscious life that helps to define what-it-is-like-to-be us. I focus here because, frankly, this is where progress is most difficult. This, then, is where progress—if there is any—will be most significant.

There is much that is relevant to my topic that I do not discuss. These lectures are already too long. I do not, for example, examine proprioception—awareness of one's own bodily states and processes—even though this is the source of some of our most obtrusive experiences (pain, hunger, thirst, etc.). What little I do say about it occurs in chapter 4, §1. This is an omission that I think could be removed without fundamental alterations to the explanatory machinery developed in chapter 1. There are, however, still other experiences—a general feeling of depression, for example—about which I do not know what to say. That is the purpose of the "plus or minus a bit" in the statement of the Representational Thesis.

The first four chapters of this book are the Nicod lectures I gave in Paris in May 1994. In these lectures I concentrated on the positive aspects of the Representational Thesis, on what it could tell us (if it were true) about self-knowledge, qualia, inverted spectra, consciousness, points of view, and the possibility of knowing what it was like to be a bat or a dogfish. There are, however, troublesome aspects to a representational approach to mental phenomena, problems that I deliberately ignored in these lectures This is especially so when representational ideas are given a naturalistic spin—see part (2) of the Representational Thesis—and applied, as I apply them, to sense experience. Many—perhaps most—philosophers are convinced that this is an area where representational ideas are *least* applicable. Even if thought, belief, and judgment can be understood as internal representations of external affairs, sensations, experiences, and feelings cannot. Unlike the conceptual side of our mental life, experiences have a phenomenal, a what-it-is-like, quality that defies representational (not to mention naturalistic) treatment. There are, furthermore, powerful intuitions—sometimes even arguments—that support this skepticism. I could not, therefore, publish these lectures without addressing these doubts. I do so in chapter 5. This concluding chapter represents my answer to those who will think, after reading chapters 1–4, that the virtues of representational naturalism are all well and good, but . . . well . . . it just can't be true. I think it can.

1 The Representational Character of Sense Experience

Sense experience is the primary locus of consciousness. Marcel (1988, p. 128) thinks that without it we would not have a concept of consciousness at all. Whether or not this is true, phenomenal experience—the look, sound, taste and feel of things—dominates our mental lives. Remove it completely and one becomes . . . what? A zombie?

If, in accordance with the Representational Thesis, we think of all mental facts as representational facts, the quality of experience, how things seem to us at the sensory level, is constituted by the properties things are represented as having. My experience of an object is the totality of ways that object appears to me, and the way an object appears to me is the way my senses represent it.

Since not all facts about representations are representational facts, and not all representations are mental, I begin by making some relevant distinctions among kinds of representations. Experience is a special kind of representation—a nonconceptual form of representation. The first order of business, then, is to say what kind of special representation this is.

I conclude the chapter with a short preview of the explanatory benefits of a representational approach to perceptual experience. In §5 I describe the way it naturalizes intentionality and in §6 the way it provides a satisfying account of why, though experiences are in the head, one doesn't find them there. Other explanatory benefits are reserved for later chapters.

1 The Nature of Representation

The fundamental idea is that a system, S, represents a property, F, if and only if S has the function of indicating (providing information about) the F of a certain domain of objects.[1] The way S performs its function (when it performs it) is by occupying different states $s_1, s_2, \ldots s_n$ corresponding to the different determinate values $f_1, f_2, \ldots f_n$, of F. A speedometer (S) represents the speed (F) of a car. Its job, its function, is to indicate, provide information (to the driver) about, how fast the car is moving (F). When it is doing its job, its different states (pointer positions "24," "37," etc.) correspond to different car speeds (24 mph, 37 mph, etc.). Given the function of this instrument, each of its states is supposed to carry a different piece of information about the speed of the car: a registration of "37" is supposed to carry the information that the car is going 37 mph, "24" the information it is going 24 mph, and so on. The fact that the speedometer has a speed indicating function, and the fact that pointing at "37" means 37 mph are representational facts about the instrument and this state of the instrument. This is what the instrument was designed to do, what it is supposed to do, and, like any fallible system, it can fail to do what it is supposed to do. If a registration of "37" on a properly installed instrument fails to carry information about the speed of the car, or carries the same information that a registration of "24" carries, then it is not doing its job. The result, often enough, is misrepresentation.

The fact that the speedometer is connected to the axle by a cable that transmits information about speed, on the other hand, is not a representational fact about this instrument. It is a fact about a representational system, but it is not a representational fact. The instrument couldn't do its job without this cable, but the fact that there is such a cable does not imply that the device *has* a job—let alone has the job of providing information. For the same reason, the fact that a particular thermometer is filled with mercury, a metal whose volume serves to indicate temperature, is a fact about a representational device, but it is not a representational fact. A representational fact about S is a fact about what S is designed to do, a fact about what information it is supposed to carry. There are facts about representations—facts about their color, shape, material constitution, and mode of operation—that do not tell one anything about what information they are supposed to supply or, indeed, whether they are supposed to supply information at all.

On the representational account of mind I intend to give, the difference between representational facts and (mere[2]) facts about representations is the difference between the mind and the brain. Neuroscientists may know a great many facts about the brain. These facts may even turn out to be facts about mental representations—facts about experiences and thoughts. That does not make knowledge of such facts knowledge of the mind. Knowledge of the mind, of mental facts, is, according to the Representational Thesis, knowledge of representational facts, not (merely) facts about mental representations. One does not understand more about the representational life of a system by being told it contains mercury or has an orange pointer. Nor does one know what (or whether) a system represents by being told that it supplies information about speed. It is not whether it supplies information about speed that is important; it is whether it has the function of doing so.

Representation is here being understood to combine teleological with information-theoretic ideas. If the concept of representation is to do a useful job in cognitive science, if it is to be used, in particular, to illuminate the nature of thought and experience, it must be rich enough to allow for misrepresentation. It must include the power to get things wrong, the power to say that something is so when it is not so. This is what the teleology, the idea of something having an information-carrying function, is doing in the present theory. It captures the normative element inherent in the idea of representation. Since an object can retain a function even when it fails to perform it (think of the heart, the kidneys, and damaged instruments), a device can retain its indicator function—continue to represent (i.e., misrepresent) something as going 34 mph, for instance—even when things go wrong, even when it fails to provide the information it is its job to provide. There is information without functions, but there is no representation without functions.

Not all events that carry information have the function of carrying it. To use Matthen's (1988) example, the angle a column of smoke makes with the horizon carries information about wind speed, but that, surely, is not the function of the smoke. The smoke cannot misrepresent wind speed. We may be misled by the column of smoke. We may take it to indicate something it doesn't (thus ourselves misrepresenting wind speed), but the smoke does not misrepresent wind speed the way an anemometer can. This, incidentally, is why black-and-white television does not misrepresent the color of the sky while color television sometimes does. The power of the color television to misrepresent color lies in its color-depicting function. The images on the two screens can be identical; yet, one misrepresents, the other does not. This is the difference between *not* representing color and *mis*representing color.

Something like this conception of representation is, I think, operative in many scientific approaches to mental representation. The terminology is not always the same, but the intuitions and theoretical purposes are similar. Anne Treisman (1992, p. 227), for example, speaks of representations as signals or events which have been assigned the "burden" (function?) of carrying meaning (information?). David Marr's (1982) well-known theory of vision assigns to early vision the function or task (Shapiro 1993) of depicting the spatial and chromatic properties of distal scenes. Gallistel (1990) describes the brain as representing aspects of the environment when there is a functioning isomorphism between the environment and the brain process that "adapts" the animal's behavior to it. Sensory organs and mechanisms are commonly described in terms of what they are "for." The semicircular canals of the middle ear are said to be for the detection of angular acceleration, the utricle and saccule for indication of linear acceleration, and the retina for encoding information about light for transmission to the brain. This way of describing perceptual mechanisms and processes is a representational way of thinking about them. The senses yield representations of the world, not just because they (when working right) deliver information about the world, but because that is their job. The senses, and the states they produce by way of performing their function, are thus evaluable in terms of how well they do their job.

Before applying these representational ideas to mental affairs, though, we need to know, in more precise terms, exactly what kind of representation a mental representation

is supposed to be. If it is, indeed, the job of the various senses to provide information about the world—thus, on the
present account, representing that world—what is the
source of these functions, what information is it their job to
provide, and how—in representational terms—do our experiences of objects differ from our thoughts about them?
What, furthermore, is it about certain representations that
makes the systems in which they occur *conscious* of what is
being represented? Good questions. I begin my answers by
explaining a number of pivotal distinctions: (1) natural vs.
conventional representations; (2) representational states vs.
representational systems; and (3) represented properties vs.
represented objects. Armed with these distinctions we can
give a preliminary taxonomy of mental representation and
begin the argument that conscious experience is a species of
natural representation.

2   Natural and Conventional Representations

The function of a system (or state) is what it is designed to
do—what it is, by design, supposed to do. There are different sources of design. Each gives rise to a different kind of
function and, thus, a different form of representation. One
important difference (for our purposes) is the difference
between naturally acquired and conventionally assigned
functions—hence, the difference between natural and conventional representations.

The information-providing functions of measuring
instruments, sensors, detectors and gauges are functions
they get from us—their makers and users. We design them.
We give them a job to do. We arrange things so that certain
liquids, by their placement in transparent tubes adjacent to a
calibrated scale, provide us with information about temper-

ature. We call the resulting artifacts thermometers. Flag poles and (metal) paper clips, the volumes of which are proportional to temperature, also carry information about temperature. Their volume is also reliably correlated with temperature. That, though, is not their function. That is not what they are designed to do. As the names suggest, they have quite a different job. Though they carry the same information, flag poles and paper clips do not represent what thermometers represent. They do not represent anything. We haven't given them that kind of job.

When a thing's informational functions are derived from the intentions and purposes of its designers, builders, and users in this way, I call the resulting representations *conventional*. Representations that are not conventional are *natural*.

I assume that there are naturally acquired functions and, thus, natural representations.[3] I do not argue for this; I assume it. This view, I know, is not universally accepted (Dennett 1987, especially pp. 287–321 and Searle 1992, p. 52, for example, deny it). I return to this point in chapter 5, but for the present I follow the lead of Wright (1983, 1987), Kitcher (1993), Godfrey-Smith (1994), Millikan (1984), Neander (1991a, 1991b), Papineau (1993), Bennett (1976) and many others in supposing that bodily organs and mechanisms can, in the relevant sense, be designed to do a certain job—and, thus, have the function of doing it—without being designed by anyone to do it. Philip Kitcher (1993, p. 380) puts it thus: "one of Darwin's important discoveries is that we can think of design without a designer." The senses, I assume, have information-providing functions, biological functions, they derive from their evolutionary history.[4] As a result, perceptual (including proprioceptive) systems produce representations of those conditions (external or internal as the case may be) they have the function of informing about. The representations they produce by way of carrying out their informational functions have a content, something they say or mean, that does not depend on the existence of our purposes and intentions. This is why the senses—or, more precisely, the internal states (experiences, feelings) the senses produce by way of performing their function—have original intentionality, something they represent, say, or mean, that they do not get from us. That is why the perceptual representations in biological systems—unlike those in laptop computers, speedometers, and television sets—make the systems in which they occur *conscious of* the objects they represent.[5]

We have, then, the following preliminary classification.

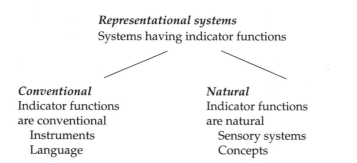

Representational systems
Systems having indicator functions

Conventional
Indicator functions
are conventional
    Instruments
    Language

Natural
Indicator functions
are natural
    Sensory systems
    Concepts

Hereafter, when speaking of the Representational Thesis, I will mean the thesis that all mental states are *natural* representations. This makes the thesis a form of philosophical naturalism.

3   Representational Systems and Representational States

The above classification is crude. All mental representations (not to mention nonmental natural representations[6]) are classified together. Thoughts and beliefs are classified with experiences. This is correct, as far as it goes. Both are forms of natural representation. For our purposes, though, it is important to distinguish seeing and hearing from knowing and believing. I can see Paul playing the piano and believe he is playing the piano, but the visual experience represents the piano playing in much different ways than does the belief. These are different kinds of mental representation. One can see or hear a piano being played without believing a piano is being played, and one can believe a piano is being played without seeing or hearing it being played. Seeing a piano being played is constituted, in part, by a visual experience, hearing by an auditory experience. Until these experiences occur one has not seen or heard the piano.[7] Experiences of piano playing do not require the concept of a piano (at least not in the same way as a belief or judgment requires it). They require no understanding of what a piano is or what it sounds like. Even mice can see and hear pianos being played.

Believing is something else. It requires the concept of a piano, some understanding of what a piano is. Mice who hear pianos being played do not believe pianos are being played. Their understanding is, I assume, too feeble to believe this even though their hearing is good enough to hear it.

All representations are representations of (purported) fact, but not all such representations are *conceptual* representations. A conceptual awareness of facts—a belief, judgment, or knowledge that the toast is burning—has a close tie with behavior. For those who have language, it normally brings with it an ability to *say* what one is aware of—that the toast is burning. This is not so with sensory awareness. One can see or smell (and, thus, be perceptually aware of) burning toast while having little or no understanding of what toast is or what it means to burn. "What is that strange smell?" might be the remark of someone who smells the toast burning but is ignorant of what toast is and what it means to burn. A mouse in the kitchen (the one who heard the piano being played) can smell, and thus have sensory awareness of burning toast but it will not (like the cook) be aware (i.e., believe) that toast is burning. The mouse will have little or no conceptual awareness of this event. It will smell the toast burning but not smell that it is, not smell it *as*, burning. The cook and the mouse differ in what they think about what they smell. They differ in how they regard the smell. They may also differ in how the burning toast smells to them. But they both smell it. They both experience it. They both have some kind of sensory representation of this event.[8]

The difference between experiences of k (as F) and thoughts about k (that it is F)—between sensory and conceptual representations of k—is generally clear enough when we describe ourselves as conscious of concrete objects (e.g., burning toast) and events (e.g., piano playing). When, however, we start describing ourselves as being aware of abstract objects—differences, numbers, answers, problems, sizes, colors—an ambiguity appears. I take a moment, therefore, to remark on this ambiguity since it would otherwise muddy the discussion to follow.

When we use an abstract noun or phrase to describe what we see, hear, or feel—what we are aware or conscious of—what is being described is normally a conceptual awareness of some (unspecified) fact. The abstract noun phrase stands in for some factive clause (Dretske 1993). Thus, to describe someone as seeing (being conscious of) the difference between A and B is to imply that the person sees (is conscious) *that* they differ. To describe someone as being aware of the color of his (blue) shirt is to imply that he or she is aware *that* the shirt is blue—thus representing the color in some conceptual way (as blue, the color of the sky, etc.) It would be odd to describe a person as seeing (thus being aware) of the color of his shirt if the person did not, at some conceptual level, know what color the shirt was. Likewise, to be aware of the problem it isn't enough to see (experience) the thing that is the problem (e.g., a clogged drain). One has to see (the fact) that it is clogged. One has to conceptualize what one sees, the clogged drain, *as* a problem. Until one conceptualizes it this way, one is not (as we say) aware of the problem.

These differences are important in thinking about ways of representing properties and, thus, according to a representational theory, the properties we are conscious of. Since the topic is our experience of objects, not our beliefs about them, we must be careful not to describe an experience of a shirt's color as an awareness or consciousness of the shirt's color. For this form of words implies[9] a conceptual representation of the shirt's color, and this may not be present. A child or an animal might be visually aware of the shirt's color (their visual experience of the shirt being, as they say, suffused with blueness) without their knowing or thinking that the shirt is blue—without sorting (or having any disposition to sort) the shirt with other blue objects. If this is hard to imagine, think of the perceiver as an animal. Cats are not color blind just because they ignore differences in color.[10] One can experience blue (the shirt's color)—and, in this sense, be aware of blue—without being conceptually aware that anything is (or looks) blue.

I will try to keep these matters straight by distinguishing between sensory and conceptual representations of facts, between experiences of *k*'s blueness and beliefs or judgments that k (or something) is (or looks) blue. The word "phenomenal" is often used to describe this sensory mode of awareness, and I will sometimes use it. Phenomenal awareness is a mode of awareness that does not require—although it may, in fact, be accompanied by—conceptual awareness. One can be phenomenally conscious of a shirt's color, of a piano being played, and of burning toast without being conscious that anything is blue, that a piano is being played, or that something is burning.

What, then, in representational terms, is the basis of this ordinary—and, I hope, familiar—distinction between an experience of color, shape, and texture, and a belief or judgment about color, shape, and texture? In representational terms, what is the difference between an olfactory experience of toast burning and a belief or judgment that toast is burning?

Experiences (sensations) of burning toast and beliefs (thoughts) that toast is burning are representations, and all representations are particular (token) states or events. Nonetheless, token states have two different sources for their indicator functions. (1) A state may derive its indicator function—and, hence, its representational status—from the system of which it is a state. Call these *systemic* indicator functions (= functions$_s$) and the representations they give rise to systemic representations (= representations$_s$). If a system (e.g., a thermometer) is supposed to provide information about temperature, and ß is the state (e.g., mercury at such-and-such level) that is supposed to carry the information that the temperature is, say, 32°, then ß has the systemic function (function$_s$) of indicating a temperature of 32°. State ß therefore represents$_s$ the temperature as being 32°. (2) A token state may, on the other hand, acquire its indicator function, not from the system of which it is a state, but from the *type* of state of which it is a token. No matter what ß systemically represents (what it is, by design of the system, supposed to indicate), it might acquire (or be given) a special, or a different, indicator function. If we print the number "38" at *this* point on the scale, then each and every time the mercury reaches *this* point, it *means* that the temperature is 38°. If we print the word "DANGER" at this (and higher) points, the mercury's rising to this point signifies danger. Call such functions (functions that state types are assigned or acquire independently of their—if any—systemic functions) *acquired* indicator functions (= functions$_a$). The indicator functions$_a$ (hence, representations$_a$) of token states may be different from their systemic functions (what they represent$_s$). As we shall see, a token state might represent in both systemic and acquired ways, and what it represents$_a$ need not be what it represents$_s$.

An example should make this difference clear. Suppose we have a simple speedometer mechanism that represents vehicle speed by registering the rotation of the axle. This mechanism was designed to be used in cars equipped with different sized tires. Since (at a given speed) the axle rotates more slowly with large tires than with small tires, the manufacturer left the job of calibrating the face of the instrument up to the user. If I use the instrument in a car with normal tires, I calibrate the dial in one way. If you use larger tires, you calibrate it differently. I put the number "50" at position ß of the pointer. You put the number "60" there. When our axles are turning at a rate corresponding to a pointer position of ß, my car is going 50 mph, your car is going 60 mph. So we calibrate differently by assigning different numbers to this pointer position. Pointer position ß, this state of the system, has the same systemic function in both cars—that of indicating an axle rotation rate of N rpm. It nonetheless, via different calibration, has a different acquired function in our two cars. In my car state ß represents$_a$ 50 mph, in your car it represents$_a$ 60 mph. State ß has the same indicator function$_s$ in all cars; what it represents$_a$ (about speed), however, varies from car to car.

To suggest (by way of tendentious description) the way this distinction is to be applied, we can describe individual systems in which this "perceptual" mechanism is installed as having the same "experiences" (viz., of an axle rotation of N) but as having different "belief's" (about speed). ß represents$_s$ (i.e., is an experience of) the same thing in all cars: an axle rotation of N. That is what this state means, what it represents$_s$, in both your car and my car. Given the information (about axle rotation) this system has the function of supplying, what it was designed (at the factory) to do, this particular state of the system has the *systemic* function of indicating an. axle rotating at N rpm. Nonetheless, although this state represents$_s$ the same thing in both systems, it represents$_a$ something different in my car than it does in your car. It represents$_a$ 50 mph in my car, 60 mph in your car. Once calibrated, my speedometer, as it were, "sees" an axle rotation of N rpm as a speed of 50 mph. Your speedometer, differently calibrated, "sees" the same thing—an axle rotation of N— but sees it *as* 60 mph. Our speedometers have the same "experience" but the experience gives rise to different "beliefs."

Walker (1983, p. 246) describes two of Pavlov's dogs. One is conditioned to salivate when middle C is played on any instrument. The other is conditioned to salivate to a clarinet playing any note. Now imagine the two dogs hearing a clarinet playing middle C. They hear the same sound. Their experience of this sound may well be the same. Their response is also the same: both salivate. Yet, their responses are mediated by different acquired representations. As a result of different learning, the dogs hear it differently—one (as we, not the dogs, might put it) hears it as middle C, the other as the sound of a clarinet. The way their experience represents$_s$ the sound may well be the same, but the way their experience represents$_a$ it is different.

As my description of these examples is intended to suggest, experiences are to be identified with states whose representational properties are *systemic*. Thought (conceptual states in general), on the other hand, are states whose representational properties are *acquired*. As a result, experiences have their representational content fixed by the biological functions of the sensory systems of which they are states.[11] How an experience represents$_s$ the world is fixed by the functions of the system of which it is a state. The quality of a sensory state—how things look, sound, and feel at the most basic (phenomenal) level—is thus determined phylogenetically. Since we inherit our sensory systems, since they are (at a fairly early age, anyway) hard-wired, we cannot (not easily anyway) change the representational$_s$ character of experience.[12] Through learning, I can change what I believe when I see k, but I can't much change the way k looks (phenomenally) to me, the kind of visual experience k produces in me. Experiences are, for this reason, modular in Fodor's (1983) sense. The way a belief represents the world, on the other hand, is ontogenetically determined. We can, through learning, change our calibration. We can change what we see something *as*—what we, upon seeing it, take it to be—even if we cannot, not in the same way, change what we see. This is why a representation$_s$ of k as red (a sensation of redness) is different from a representation$_a$ of k as red (a belief that k is red) even though both are representations of k as red.

The above example is a bit too simple-minded to reveal the full power of the represented$_s$-represented$_a$ distinction to illuminate the sensation-cognition (experience-belief) difference. Perhaps, therefore, a minor embellishment will better reveal its potential for capturing some of the structure of actual sensory systems (I am thinking mainly of constancy mechanisms).

Another manufacturer produces a more sophisticated speedometer. It is designed to be used on all cars, no matter what size tires they use. Pointer positions are determined by two sources of information: not just by the rate at which the axle is rotating, but by the height of the axle above the road surface. Since the height of the axle above the road surface provides a useful measure of tire size, these two sources of information are combined to yield a reliable measure of car speed no matter what size tires are used. The pointer positions of these instruments—driven by two sources of information—thus have a speed-indicating systemic function and are therefore calibrated at the factory. As their construction suggests, these more sophisticated instruments are designed to provide information, not about how fast the axle is rotating, but about how fast the car is going. Although the information-handling processes in these fancy instruments use information about axle rotation to generate a representation of speed, the final representation (pointer position) does not, in fact, indicate how fast the axle is rotating. The early phase in this informational process uses information about axle-rotation, but (by integrating it with information about elevation) it sacrifices this information in order to produce a final indication of speed. Information about axle rotations is thereby lost. This is an instrument whose individual states (pointer positions) represent$_s$ speed, not axle rotation. This instrument, unlike the crude one described above, "experiences" speed (not axle rotation) even though the information-delivery process depends on information about axle rotation to generate this "experience."

But if speed is what this instrument "experiences" (= what its various states have the systemic function of indicating) what does it "believe"? This depends on what the states of this instrument represent$_a$, what they have acquired (or been assigned[13]) the job of indicating. Normally, of course, if the instrument was to be used as a speedometer, one would assign functions to its various states in the way that reflected their systemic functions. The state, ß, having the function$_s$ of indicating a speed of 50 mph, would be given this function$_a$ by printing the number "50" at this position of the pointer.[14] We are, however, free to assign any functions$_a$ we please. If we aren't particularly interested in exactly how fast the car is going, we could partition the dial into several sub-divisions and label them "slow," "medium," and "fast." Then ß (having the function$_s$ of indicating a speed of 50 mph) gets the same function$_a$ as the state _ (having the function$_s$ of indicating a speed of 48 mph)—the function$_a$, namely, of indicating a *medium* speed. This, in fact, might be the functions these states acquire if we used the device, not as a speedometer, but as a mechanism to control an automatic transmission. In this case, since we want the car to be in 3d gear at both 48 mph and 50 mph, we give these two states the same function$_a$. If the various states of the device acquire *these* functions$_a$, then it will end up "experiencing" 50 mph and 48 mph (these are the speeds these two states represent$_s$), but representing$_a$ them both in the same way (as a 3d gear speed). It experiences a difference between 50 mph and 48 mph, yes, but it, so to speak, "sees" both these speeds as medium (or 3d gear) speeds. Conceptually, this system "abstracts" from the sensory difference between 48 and 50 mph.

The last example is meant to be suggestive of the way innate sensory systems might have the function of delivering information about more or less continuous quantities (surface reflectances, speed, direction, frequency, etc.) while the cognitive system might "chunk" this information into parcels that are more useful to the individual system's needs and purposes. At the level of experience, I am sensitive to (i.e., can discriminate) all manner of differences in the light, sound, pressure, temperature, and chemistry of objects affecting my senses. I nonetheless have a limited conceptual repertoire for categorizing these sensory differences, for making judgments about (= representations$_a$ of) the differences I experience. I experience the differences (in the same way the speedometer described above registers a difference between 50 mph and 48 mph), but, at the conceptual level, I treat these differences as different instances of the same kind. At the sensory level I can discriminate hundreds of different colors. At the conceptual level I operate with, at best, a few dozen categories for the colors I experience. Learning calibrates me no more finely than I need to satisfy needs and carry out purposes. This is not to say, of course, that I could not "recalibrate" in a more discriminating way if the need arose. The information needed for such recalibration is already there in my experience.

The taxonomy, then, looks like this:

Representations
States having indicator functions

Conventional
Conventional functions

Natural
Natural functions

Sensory
States with systemic
indicator functions
  Experiences
  Sensations
  Feelings

Conceptual
States with acquired
indicator functions
  Thoughts
  Judgments
  Beliefs

A few clarificatory remarks are in order:

(a) Experiences are representations$_s$, but, as noted earlier, not all representations$_s$ (not even all natural representations$_s$) are mental—let alone experiences. Experiences are those natural representations$_s$ that service the construction of representations$_a$, representations$_s$ that can be calibrated (by learning) to more effectively service an organism's needs and desires. They are the states whose functions it is to supply information to a cognitive system for calibration and use in the control and regulation of behavior.[15] Evans (1982, chapter 7, §4) expresses a similar idea when he describes internal states whose content depends on their phylogenetically ancient connections with the motor system. In order to qualify as conscious experiences, Evans requires that these content-bearing states serve as input to what he calls a "concept-exercising and reasoning system."[16] This is why, in our (second) speedometer example, the early stages in the information-delivery process (the ones carrying information about axle rotation, for example) are not appropriate analogues of experience. Though these early processes have a function$_s$—that of providing information about axle rotation (information the system needs to generate a representation of speed)—and therefore represent$_s$ axle rotation, this information is not available for calibration. The instrument *uses* this information, but doesn't, so to speak, make it available to calibrational (cognitive) processes. There is, then, no way this information can be given "conceptual" form. The information vanishes (absorbed into information about speed) before it reaches the relevant control structures that determine behavior (in this case, pointer positions). These are natural representations$_s$ that are not mental. Their function is to supply information to representations$_s$ that are.[17]

(b) Sensory systems have phylogenetic functions and are, therefore, comparatively modular in Fodor's (1983) sense: hard-wired, informationally incapsulated, and so on. This is not to say that the states (experiences) they produce are immune to changes in their representational status. We can use a pressure gauge (function$_s$ = delivering information about pressure) as an altimeter by recalibrating its face in "feet above sea level." Pointer positions representing$_s$ pressure now (also) represent$_a$ altitude. The gauge, as it were, experiences pressure *as* altitude. This same transformation occurs as we learn to identify and recognize objects and conditions we experience. We begin by hearing (experiencing) sounds and end by hearing (recognizing) words. We still hear sounds, of course, but, after learning, after the kind of calibration occurs that is involved in language learning, experiences acquire an added representational dimension.[18]

Sensory adaptation may be an instance of such recalibration. Just as we can recalibrate a speedometer when we change the size of our tires (the state ß acquiring the function of indicating a speed of 60 mph, not, as it did with normal tires, a speed of 50 mph) so also can sensory systems recalibrate when there is a change in the information an experience delivers. After wearing spectacles that make everything "look" 30° to the left, touch "educates" vision and objects begin to "look" to be where they can be grasped. This, at least, is one way of describing the experiential change that accompanies adaptation. As we age, there is a gradual yellowing of the macula (spot on the retina) that changes the signals sent from the retina to the brain about the wavelength of light (example taken from Clark 1993, p. 170). Despite this constant change in the information representational$_s$ states carry, there is no corresponding representational$_a$ change: we still see blue and yellow, red and green, *as* blue and yellow, red and green.

(c) The states by means of which a representational system performs its informational functions have a structure that enables them to acquire functions without explicitly acquiring them. Once we assign "12" to a certain position of the clock hands, all the remaining indicator states (positions of the clock hands) receive an "implied" indicator function. When there is this kind of structure among a system's indicator states (as there is in our experience of color and sound, for instance), there is no reason to suppose that *each* representational$_s$ state has explicitly obtained its indicator function through some distinguishable evolutionary process. All the indicator states may receive an implied indicator function by one state explicitly acquiring it.

(d) Audition provides information, not only about pitch and intensity, but about timbre and (binaurally) the directional properties of sound. In the case of vision, there seems to be separate pathways, different systems, for information about color, location, form, and movement (Fischback 1992, p. 56; Zeki 1992, p. 71).

It would be more appropriate, then, to describe a given sense modality, not (as I have been doing) as having the function of indicating F, but as having multiple indicator functions. And there is no reason experiences "associated" with a given sense modality (smell or vision) might not exploit information from other modalities (see, e.g., Stein and Meredith 1993; Dretske 1981, pp. 145–147).

(e) Finally, the subjective quality of an experience, the phenomenal appearances, are the way experience represents$_s$ things to be. If I can use the speedometer analogy again, the first speedometer has axle-rotation qualia. The second has speed qualia. Once calibrated, though, both "describe" (i.e., represent$_a$) how things seem to them in the same way—as a vehicle speed of so-and-so many miles per hour. If we are talking about vehicle speed, things *seem* the same to them.

I am, with these brief remarks, trying to indicate how I intend to use the distinction between systemic and acquired representations. Justification for thinking of experience and thought in this way will come later. I am quite aware that questions about qualia, about what it is like to have an experience, about the way things seem, are complex questions that, often enough, straddle the sensation-cognition fence. We are sometimes talking about the properties objects are represented$_s$ as having (the phenomenal appearances), at other times about the ones they are represented$_a$ as having (what the phenomenal appearances prompt us to believe, or what we, on the basis of the experience, are inclined to take something as). I return to these tangled issues in chapters 3 and 5.[19]

4   Represented Properties and Represented Objects

Ordinary thermometers represent the temperature of whatever medium they are in. Put one in your coffee and it tells you how hot your coffee is. Hang the same thermometer on the wall and it tells you the temperature of the room. Put it in your mouth and it indicates something about you—whether you have a fever. It isn't the function of this instrument to say what it is—coffee, living room, or you—whose temperature it registers. The instrument says how hot *this* is, where *this* is whatever medium the thermometer is in. It does not represent the relationship (i.e., its being *in* this) that makes it *this* rather than *that* it represents the temperature of.

The same is true of all representational devices. Pressure gauges do not tell you which (if any) tire it is that they represent the pressure of. If you want to know which tire (if any) the gauge represents, which topic it is commenting on, you have to look, not at the gauge, but at the external connections between gauge and world that make it the right front tire, not the left rear tire, whose pressure it registers. Gauges do not supply—they do not have the function of supplying—information about these external connections. Representations have a sense (the properties they have the function of indicating) and, often enough, a reference (an object whose properties they represent), but the sense does not determine the reference. Two representations with the same sense can have different referents.

The difference between represented object and represented property, between the reference and the sense of a representation, is the same distinction Nelson Goodman (1976) was getting at in his contrast between a picture of a black horse ("black horse" here specifying the object the picture is a picture of) and a black-horse picture ("black-horse" here specifying what the picture depicts the object as). Some pictures of black horses do not represent the black horse as a black horse. They are not black-horse pictures. Imagine taking a picture of a black horse at a great distance. The picture depicts the black horse as, say, a spot in the distance. It could be anything. Or imagine taking a picture of a black horse disguised to look like a brown camel. This picture of a black horse is a brown-camel picture. Others (e.g., Lloyd 1989, p. 14) make the same distinction by contrasting explicit with extensional content. The extensional content is what object it is that is being represented. The explicit content is the way this object is being represensted—as a so-and-so. The object a representation is a representation of is not determined by the properties that object is represented as having. Nothing guarantees that black-horse pictures are pictures of black horses.

Experiences are like pictures in this regard; they are *de re* modes of representation (Burge 1977; Bach 1986, 1987; Recanati 1993). Although token experiences may be individuated by being experiences of a particular object, k, tokens of the same experience type can occur with a different k or with no object at all (hallucinations, dreams, imagination). Although my present black-horse experience is an experience of a black horse (I am, that is, seeing a black horse), I can nonetheless have exactly the same type of experience, a black-horse experience, without its being an experience of a black horse or, indeed, an experience of any object at all.[20] What determines the reference for a *de re* mode of representation (the object it is a representation of) is not *how* it is represented, but a certain external causal or contextual relation I will designate as C.[21] There is nothing in the content of the representation, nothing the representation *says*, which makes it about this object rather than that object or no object at all. *De re* modes of representation have their reference determined contextually, by the relation I am here calling C. Since the veridicality of an experience depends on its reference—on what object (if any) it is an experience of—the veridicality of experience is determined, in part, by context (C). C makes it the case that k is the object S represents as blue. C thereby helps to determine whether the representation (that k is blue) is veridical or not. Nonetheless, the fact that it is k (rather than some other object or no object at all) that stands in relation C to the representation is not what the representation represents. Representations do not (indeed, cannot) represent context. They represent k as being blue, but they do so without representing it to be k that they represent to be blue.

The speedometer in my car is connected to the axle of my car, not your car. It therefore represents (or misrepresents, as the case may be) the speed of my car, not your car. It is in virtue of this special relation, C, to my car that it can do what other speedometers cannot do—viz., say something (whether truly or falsely) about my car. Other speedometers cannot even say something false about my car. C is the relation such that, when a representational system S is functioning properly, and k stands in C to S, then S will indicate the F of k. If k is the object whose F is represented at time t, then we can say that, at time t, S represents k. At other times S may be deployed differently—thus, at different times, representing different objects. Changing the way a system is deployed, changing the object that stands in relation C to S, changes what S represents (what *object* it represents), but not necessarily what S says (represents) about it.

As I am using terms, then, the fact that S represents k is not—at least not a pure—representational fact about S. It is a fact about a representation—an important fact for many practical purposes—but it is not a fact that has to do exclusively with what the system has the function of indicating. S has the function of indicating the F of those objects which stand in C to it, but it does not have the job of indicating—does not therefore represent—which objects—or even whether there is an object—that stands in C to it. When we describe S (whose function it is to indicate F) as representing k, this implies that, for some F, S represents (possibly misrepresents) the F of k. That S represents k, therefore, implies a representational fact—that, for some F, S represents the F of k. But it also implies something that is not a representational fact—viz., that k stands in relation C to S. So facts about the object of representation are *hybrid* facts—part representational, part not. This will be important when we discuss (in chapter 2) introspective knowledge. For what is known by introspection are mental—hence, (according to the Representational Thesis) representational—facts. Hybrid representational facts (that S represents k) are mixtures of representational facts and facts about representations. This is why one cannot know, at least not by introspection, what object (or whether there is an object) one is experiencing.[22]

Clearly, then, my use of the word "something" in the description of S as representing something as being blue is not an existential quantifier. It may turn out that S is misrepresenting something to be F when there is something (in the next room, say) that *is* F. The fact that there is something in the world that is going 25 mph does not mean that a speedometer registering "25 mph" says something true about the world. For what the speedometer "says" is not that there is something in the world going 25 mph, but that *this* (whatever it is that stands in C to the instrument) is going 25 mph. If representational system S says anything at all when it represents color—and, thus, represents something as being (say) blue—it is that *this* is blue where *this* is whatever object (if there is one) to which S stands in the C-relation. If there is no object of representation, then, S represents (i.e., misrepresents) *this* as being blue when there is no *this*. If we take this to mean that, owing to a failure of presupposition, what S represents to be so (the content of the representation) is neither true nor false, this merely shows something about the nature of sense experience that we knew all along: viz., that misrepresentation takes two forms. An experience can misrepresent by (1) saying something false, by saying that *this* is blue when *it* (the object of representation) is not blue, and (2) by saying what is neither true nor false—that *this* is blue when there is no "this" that is not blue. When there is no object of representation, nothing that S represents to be blue, I shall continue to describe S as representing something to be blue. It should be understood, however, that when there is no object, "something" stands in for a failed indexical.

We thus have two different kinds of misrepresentation:

S represents color
S represents something to be (say) blue

Object of representation
There is an object S
represents to be blue

No object of representation
There is no object S
represents to be blue

Veridical
The object S
represents to
be blue is blue

Misrepresentation
The object S
represents to be
blue is not blue

Misrepresentation
S represents something
to be blue, but there is
no object that S represents to be blue

5   Intentionality

Brentano (1874) conjectured that a mark of the mental was intentionality. Whatever, exactly, Brentano meant by intentionality, and whether or not he was right about its being a feature of all, and only, mental events, most philosophers take intentional characteristics (variously understood) to be distinctive of a great many mental phenomena. What follows is a brief catalog of those aspects of intentionality that have figured most prominently in the recent literature. In each case we find that a representational account of the mind provides a satisfying explanation of intentionality. By conceiving of mental facts—and, in particular, those about sense experience—as part of the natural order, as manifestations of overall biological and developmental design, one can see where intentionality comes from and why it is there. In each case, intentionality is real enough, but it turns out, as Fodor (1987) suggests it must, to be really something else.

1. *The Power to Misrepresent* Chisholm (1957) describes this as the first mark of intentionality. Beliefs and experiences have the power to "say" or "mean" that k is F when k is not F. Indeed, they have the power to say this (see above) even when there is no k. If we understand representations as states having indicator functions (systemic or acquired), we can understand where they get this power. Unlike symbols, diagrams, gauges, and instruments, moreover, it is a power that natural representations do not get from us. They are states that exhibit the first mark of intentionality in an original (nonderived) form.

2. *Aboutness* This, of course, is the power or capacity of one state of affairs to refer to or be about another. S sees Tom, hears him, has thoughts about him and desires for him. These are things S cannot do unless S occupies states that

have Tom as their object, as what they refer to, as what they are thoughts *about*, experiences *of*, and desires *for*. In seeing Tom, S's experiences of Tom may not depict who (or what) it is they are experiences of. S can, after all, see Tom on a foggy night and mistake him for someone else. But if Tom stands in the right causal relationship to these experiences, they are experiences of him. Echoing Goodman, S's experience need not be a Tom-experience in order to be an experience *of* Tom.

We not only experience and think about objects, we also experience and think about their properties. I see a golf ball and, in seeing it, I experience its color, shape, movement, and dimpled texture. My experience is of or about these properties as much as it is of the golf ball. I could be experiencing these properties (during a dream or hallucination) when there was no golf ball, no object that had the properties I experience. Whether or not there is an object, the experience is still an experience of whiteness, roundness, movement, and texture.

Even the simplest measuring instruments exhibit these dimensions of aboutness albeit in a derived way. In representing the pressure in an intake manifold, a pressure gauge "says" something about the manifold. It is not only about the manifold (an object), it is about the pressure in it (a property) and, therefore, about the manifold's having that pressure (a condition or state). If pressure gauges were conscious, if their intentionality was original rather than conventional, the manifold (the one standing in relation C to the gauge) would be the object the gauge was conscious of, having a pressure of 14 psi would be the property the gauge perceived it to have, and its having a pressure of 14 psi would be the condition, state of affairs, or fact the gauge was aware of.

Though *aboutness* is here being understood in terms of the reference of a representational state, and reference, in turn, is fixed by contextual relation C, this should not be taken to mean that this dimension of intentionality is being equated with a causal or informational relation (whatever the relation C comes down to) between two objects. What makes S *about* the object *k* is not simply the fact that *k* stands in relation C to S. Standing in relation C to S is necessary, but not sufficient, to make S about *k*. The system to which *k* stands in this relation must be a *representational* system, one having the *function* of indicating the F of those objects which stand in C to it. If S did not have this function, if there wasn't something S was *supposed* to indicate about *k*, then even if *k* stood in relation C to S, S would not be about *k*. A playground teeter-totter's position stands in the same relation to the children playing on it that a beam balance stands to the objects whose weights it has the function to compare. The behavior of the balance "says" or represents something about the objects on it. It "says" that one is heavier than the other. The teeter-totter does not. This is not to say that we could not *learn* something (exactly what we learn from the balance) about the relative weight of the children from the behavior of the teeter-totter. This, though, doesn't make the teeter-totter's state *about* the children in any relevant sense of "about." A drunk's behavior is not *about* his blood chemistry just because we can use his behavior to tell something about the chemistry of his blood.

3. *Aspectual Shape* In thinking about a ball I think about it in one way rather than another—as red not blue, as round not square, as stationary not moving. These are the aspects under which I think of the ball. I can desire an apple, yes, but in desiring an apple I desire to eat it, taste it, throw it, hold it, look at it, or simply have it. These are the aspects

(the language of "aspects" is taken from Searle 1992) under which I desire the apple. Our mental states not only have a reference, an aboutness, an object (or purported object) that forms their topic; they represent that object in one way rather than another. When an object is represented, there is always an aspect under which it is represented. Even when there is no object, the *aspect* remains.

The same is true of the objects we experience. The objects I see *look* a certain way to me—red, round, and stationary. The objects I touch feel a certain way to me—rough and cold. Experiences are of objects, yes, but one cannot experience an object without experiencing it under some aspect. This follows immediately from the fact that the experienced object is simply that object, if there is one, whose determinable properties the sensory system represents. One cannot, therefore, see, smell, or taste an object without experiencing it as having determinate properties.

Aspects come finely individuated and this, too, is part of what is meant in speaking of aspectual shape. If we suppose that, in accordance with gas laws, the pressure of the gas in a (constant volume) tank cannot be 14 psi without the gas having a temperature of (say) 38°C, an instrument cannot help delivering information about temperature (that the gas is 38°C) in delivering information about pressure (that it is 14 psi). It can, nonetheless, *represent* the one without representing the other. An instrument can have a pressure-indicating function without having a temperature-indicating function even when it cannot deliver information about pressure without delivering information about temperature. A pressure gauge is not a thermometer just because it delivers information about temperature (though we could certainly use it as, and therefore make it, one). Doing X doesn't automatically give you the function of doing X, and having the function of providing temperature information is what is needed to represent temperature. It is the specificity of indicator functions to *this* property rather than *that* property (even when the properties are nomically correlated) that explains the aspectual profile of representations and, therefore (according to the Representational Thesis) the aspectual character of experience and thought.[23] It is the explanation for why experiencing a certain pressure is different from experiencing a certain temperature even when these aspects cannot be separated in the object one experiences.

4. *Directedness* The objective reference of an experience—what object the experience is an experience of—is a relational, a contextual, property of the experience. Two experiences can be subjectively indistinguishable, both be black-horse experiences, and, yet, one be an experience of a black horse, the other not. Directedness, on the other hand, is supposed to be a quality of experience that is supposed to be intrinsic to the experience. It is supposed to be part of what it is like to have that experience. If I understand it (and I'm not sure I do) it is the quality of experience by means of which experience purports to refer to some object or fact. Experiences are supposed to exhibit this kind of intentionality—directedness—whether or not they have an objective referent, whether or not they are about something in the sense described above. Miller (1984) explains Husserl's technical term "noema" in this way:

Since an act has directedness regardless of whether or not it has an object, something other than the object must be that which accounts for the act's directedness. This "something," according to Husserl, is the act's *noema*. (16)

There is, however, a connection between the noema of an experience and its reference. Following Føllesdal (1969),

Miller (p. 17) takes the noema to be that which determines which object (if there is one) is the object of the experience. For an experience to be directed is, simply, for it to have a noema (p. 31). To say that experiences have this quality of directedness, then, is to say that they have a subjectively accessible quality that is such that if they have an objective reference (some object they are *of*), this quality determines which object it is.

If we understand directedness in this way, however, it sounds as though there is supposed to be some subjective quality of experience that is such that if I am (in fact) seeing a black horse, it determines which black horse I am seeing. If this is what directedness is supposed to be, it seems clear that experiences do not have it. When I am experiencing an object, nothing in my experience of it determines *which* object I'm experiencing anymore than there is something about a gauge's representation of a tire's pressure that determines *which* tire it is registering the pressure of. Representations are not like that. Neither are experiences.

I'm not sure, though, that I understand noema and the directedness they are supposed to confer on experiences. Miller (1984, p. 69) says that the part of the noema (or *noematic sinn*: the reference determining aspect of the noema) which determines the purported object of the act (in abstraction from properties) is indexical (also Christensen 1993, p. 758). If this means, as it seems to mean, that what object, if any, an experience is directed at is determined, not within the subjective "accessible" character of the experience itself, but by the contextual or relational properties of the experience (what I called relation "C" in §3), then, once again, directedness comes out the same as aboutness as already defined. It does not represent an additional aspect of intentionality.

Sometimes, of course, the properties being represented apply uniquely to only one object. This is especially true in vision where experience represents objects as being in particular places, places that (given the way we represent objects) can only be occupied by one object. Something is represented as being here and something is represented as being there. It does not make much sense to suppose that the object being represented as here is really being represented as *there*. I can, at a given time, represent more than one object as red so that an object's being represented as red will not determine which object (if any) I am representing. But if I represent an object as being here (where it is understood that only one object can be represented as being here), the representation of it as being here determines which object (if there is one) is being represented that way. It is the one being represented as here. If this is what directedness comes down to, then directedness has to do, not with object-reference (if any) of the experience, but with certain special properties that this purported object is represented as having. Even simple instruments can have this kind of directedness (in a derived way). Radar is "directed" at whatever object it represents as being at coordinates $[x,y,z]$. If there is an object there, the representation of it as being there, at $[x,y,z]$, determines which object it is that is being represented as being there. It is the object that is there—at $[x,y,z]$.

6   Mind and Brain: The Whereabouts of Experience

Insofar as a representational account of sense experience depicts experience as representational, it likens experience to something like a story. In thinking about a story we can be thinking about: (1) the words that tell the story or (2) what those words mean, the story they tell. Call the first the *story-vehicle* and the second the *story-content*. Stories (i.e., story vehicles) are in books, but what happens in the story (content) does not happen in a book. It need not happen anywhere. The maiden was rescued by a knight in shining armor—that episode was certainly *in* the story—but, though this story is *in* a book, no one expects to find a maiden, a knight, or a daring rescue *in* (i.e., between the covers of) a book.

Whenever one talks about representations, there is this kind of ambiguity, the ambiguity between representational vehicle and representational content. Our talk about thoughts and experiences exhibits this kind of ambiguity. In the same way that stories are in books, thoughts and experiences are in heads. What is in the head, of course, are the experience-vehicles, the physical states that have a representational-content, the states that tell (express) a story about the world—that say or mean, for example, that there is something red over here and something triangular over there. Thoughts and experiences have to be in the head (or at least somewhere in the body) if our having them is (sometimes) to explain why we act the way we do. I go to the closet because I want to get dressed and think that is where my clothes are. If my thought (that my clothes are in the closet) and desire (to get dressed) were not *in me*—at least states or conditions *of me*, how could they possibly explain my trip to the closet? The itch I feel has to be in me to explain why I scratch. If mental states are to have an explanatory role, if we sometimes do what we do because of what we think and experience, then beliefs and experiences have to be *in* the systems whose behavior they explain. Aside, though, from their role in explaining behavior (some philosophers are sceptical of this), experiences have to be in us in order to explain why, for instance, I cease to experience a room full of people when I close my eyes. The room full of people does not vanish, but something ceases to exist when I close my eyes. And this something has to be in me or a state of me. Why else would its existence be so utterly dependent on the position of my eyelids?

But though the thoughts and experiences have to be in us, we all know what we will find when we look inside the skull. If there are sensations and feelings in there, they seem to be well camouflaged. When Wilder Penfield (1957, 1959) looked into the brain of his patient, a patient who was (as a result of electrical stimulation by Penfield) experiencing a variety of sensations, he did not observe the colors and sounds the patient reported experiencing. This is exactly what one would expect on a representational theory of experience. Just as what makes a story the story it is is what it is a story about (i.e., the story-content), so what makes a mental state—and, in particular, an experience—the experience it is is what it is an experience of. We can have stories about blue dogs (blue-dog stories) and blue-dog experiences. Stories about blue dogs—the blue dog vehicles—are neither blue nor doglike. Just look in the book. It is all black and white. Just so, what we find by looking in the brain of a person experiencing blue dogs is neither blue nor doglike. We do not find the content of experience, the properties that make the experience the kind of experience it is. What we find, instead, are electrical and chemical activity in gray, cheesy brain matter. We find the experience vehicles (see Lycan 1990, p. 111; Tye 1991, p. 118, for the same point). What we find, in other words, are the same sort of thing we find when we look in books: representational vehicles that in no way resemble what these representations represent.

According to the Representational Thesis, the facts that make what is in the head mental, the facts that convert electrical and chemical activity in the cortex into blue-dog experiences, are facts that are not identifiable by looking, exclusively, at what is in the head. What makes a certain pattern of electrical activity in the cortex into a blue-dog experience is a fact about what this activity represents, what it has the function of indicating. What something represents, what it has the function of indicating, are not facts one can discover by looking *in* the cortex, *at* the representations. One could as well hope to figure out what, if anything, a voltage difference between two electrical contacts in a computer means (represents, signifies) by taking ever more exacting measurements of the voltage. One could as well hope to figure out what, if anything, ancient scratchings on a cave wall meant by peering at them with a magnifying glass. That isn't going to tell you what anything means or, indeed, whether there is meaning—content—there at all. According to the Representational Thesis, that is why looking at the brain of a person having an experience isn't going to tell you what that person is experiencing. The experience-vehicle is there, but the experience-content isn't there, and, just like stories, it is the content that makes the experience (the story) the experience (the story) it is.

What sometimes helps to obscure the difference between representation- vehicle and representation-content is a confusion (fostered by conventional measuring instruments) about how one goes about determining what a representation represents. Instruments come with their representational "faces" calibrated in degrees Fahrenheit, pounds per square inch, ohms, miles per hour, revolutions per minute, and so on. This enables users to tell, not only *what* the instrument is designed to measure, but *how* it represents that quantity. One merely looks at the representation (e.g., a pointer pointing at the numeral "900" on the face of an instrument labeled TACHOMETER and calibrated in rpm's) to discover what the instrument is "saying," what it represents, what story it is telling about the engine. Looking at the representation-vehicle, the pointer pointing at "900," tells you what the representation-content is—that the engine is turning at 900 rpm. With everything neatly labeled in this way, one can, as it were, see what the instrument is "seeing," see what its "experience" is like, by looking in (or at) the instrument. This obscures the distinction between the representation itself, something (the vehicle) that is *in* the instrument, something (the vehicle) that *tells* a story about the engine, on the one hand, and, on the other hand, what is being represented (= content), the story being told, something that is *not* in the instrument. An animal's brain doesn't come neatly labeled in this way. That is why you cannot tell, by looking at (or in) it, what the animal whose brain it is is experiencing. You couldn't do it with an instrument either without the help of labels. The representations are there, but their content is not. In this sense, the mind isn't in the head any more than stories (i.e., story contents) are in books.

2   Introspection

I think today is Wednesday. How do I know I think this? From this angle A looks longer than B. How do I know it does?

These are not questions about how I know that today is Wednesday or that A is longer than B. They are questions about how I know something about myself—of what I think and how things look to me. They are questions about what John Locke called *reflection*—the notice that the mind takes of its own operations and states. Natsoulas (1983) defines one form of consciousness—reflective consciousness—as a privileged ability to be noninferentially aware of (all or some of) one's current mental occurrences. We seem to have this ability. In telling you what I believe I do not have to figure this out (as you might have to) from what I say or do. There is nothing from which I infer that A looks longer than B. It just does. That is somehow given—knowledge the mind has of itself. I will call the mind's direct knowledge of itself introspective knowledge. Introspection is the process by means of which we come by such knowledge.

That we have introspective knowledge is obvious. Philosophers may disagree about the mode of access we have to our own thoughts and feelings and whether the authority we enjoy is that of infallibility or something less, but most are willing to concede that there is a dramatic difference between the way you know how I feel and the way I know it. The problem is to explain how we come by such knowledge and what gives us this first-person authority.

If the idea of the mind turning its attention onto itself strikes one, as it struck Wittgenstein (1974, §412) as "the queerest thing there could be" a representational theory dispels the mystery. It gives an account of introspective knowledge that is compellingly simple and plausible. There is no appeal to—no longer a need for—internal scanners monitoring the clockwork of the mind. What one comes to know by introspection are, to be sure, facts about one's mental life— thus (on a representational theory) representational facts. These facts are facts, if you will, about internal representations. The objects and events one perceives to learn these facts, however, are seldom internal and never mental.[1] One becomes aware of representational facts by an awareness of physical objects. One learns that A looks longer than B, not by an awareness of the experience that represents A as longer than B, but by an awareness of A and B, the objects the experience is an experience of. On a representational theory of the mind, introspection becomes an instance of *displaced perception*—knowledge of internal (mental) facts via an awareness of external (physical) objects.[2]

A representational theory of the mind is an externalist theory of the mind and, therefore, faces the same problems that all externalist theories confront (Boghossian 1989). If mental facts are constituted, not by the intrinsic character of the events occurring inside, but by the *relations* these internal events bear to external affairs (e.g., by their indicator function) then how is it possible to know, by "looking inward," by *intro*spection, what is going on in the mind?

That would be like trying to determine, with the aid of mirrors, whether one was a father or a citizen of the United States. This "problem" evaporates once one understands that introspection is *not* a process in which one looks inward. Even if we could look inside, there would be no point in doing so. The mental facts one seeks to discover by introspection are not there.

1   Displaced Perception

Many of the facts we come to know through ordinary sense perception are facts about objects we do not perceive.

I see how much I weigh by looking at the bathroom scale on which I stand. The object I see is the bathroom scale. The fact I learn is a fact about me—that I weigh 170 pounds. This pattern—perceptual object in one place, perceptual fact in another—is familiar. One looks at a gauge on the dashboard in order to see how much gas remains in the gas tank—a fact about an object, a tank located beneath the car, that one does not see. One listens for the sound of a timer to find out when a cake in the oven is done and reads the newspapers or watches television to see what is happening on the other side of the world. During instrument landing all the important facts are outside, but the instruments and gauges—the objects the pilot actually sees—are inside. In such cases one comes to know that k is F—sees that k is F—by seeing and hearing, not k itself, but h. The perceptual fact is displaced from the perceptual object.[3]

Perceptual displacement—seeing that k is F by seeing, not k, but some other object, h, occurs when there is conceptual, but no corresponding sensory, representation of k[4] In seeing that I have gained five pounds by looking at the bathroom scale, there is a conceptual representation of *me* as having gained five pounds, but a sensory representation of the scale, not me. The properties sensuously represented (i.e., represented$_s$) are properties of the scale (its color, orientation, size, shape, etc.), not properties of me. The property conceptually represented (i.e., represented$_a$)—having gained 5 pounds—is a property of me, not the scale.[5]

Perceptual displacement requires belief (knowledge? justified belief?[6]) that an appropriate connection exists between the properties of the perceived object (h) and the properties of the target object (k)—the object the perceptual belief is a belief about. One must believe that h would not be G unless k were (probably) F. Those who do not believe this will not see that k is F when they see that h is G. If you don't know that the object you are standing on is a scale, don't (therefore) believe that the position of its pointer indicates the weight of the person standing on it, you will not see how much you weigh by looking at it. Those who perceive h without an appropriate connecting belief (as I will call it)—a belief about the relationship between h and k—will perceive the same objects but not the same facts.

Perceptual displacement enlarges the number of facts one perceives without a corresponding enlargement in the number of objects one perceives. To expand one's observational powers, one does not need microscopes and telescopes. They help (because they increase the number and kind of objects one can see), but they aren't necessary. One can also see more facts, not by seeing more objects, but by expanding one's knowledge of what the objects one can already see signify about the objects one cannot see. This is what connecting beliefs (e.g., well-confirmed theories) provide.

Before turning to the demonstration that, on a representational theory of perception, introspective knowledge (at least of certain mental states) is a form of displaced perception, a word about the facts that introspective knowledge is knowledge of. Introspective knowledge is knowledge of the mind—i.e., mental facts. Since mental facts (according to the thesis I am promoting) are representational facts, introspective knowledge is a (conceptual) representation of a representation—of the fact that something (else) is a representation or has a certain representational content. It is, in this sense, *metarepresentational* (see Pylyshyn (1978, p. 593) and Perner (1991, p. 35)). Metarepresentations are not merely representations of representations. They are representations of them *as* representations. If we think of a photograph as a (pictorial) representation (of whomever or whatever it is a picture), we can represent this photograph in a variety of different ways. We can represent it as a piece of paper, as a piece of paper weighing 2 grams, as rectangular, and as having certain colored areas on its surface. We can also represent it as a picture of Clyde (or, simply, as *of* Clyde where "Clyde" is understood to be a description of what the picture is a picture of—its representational content). In describing it as a picture of Clyde, I represent the object as a representation. I thus produce a metarepresentation. A description of the picture as weighing 2 grams is not a metarepresentation. It represents a representation, but not *as* a representation. A picture of a picture that does not represent the picture as a picture[7] is not a metarepresentation of the picture.

Using this terminology in a different way, Lloyd (1989, p. 169), calls a metarepresentation any representation of a representation in which the representing properties (of the representation) are explicitly represented. Thus, a photocopy of this page—one that clearly identified the shape and arrangement of the letters—would be a metarepresentation according to the way I understand Lloyd. The copy would explicitly represent the properties of the symbols—their individual shapes and arrangement—by means of which they represent what they represent. The photocopy would not, however, be a metarepresentation as I am using this word. The photocopy would not represent the marks on the page *as* representing anything. That isn't the function of the picture. Its function is to copy the symbols on the page whether or not they are meaningful. It will copy gibberish as faithfully as meaningful prose.

Introspective knowledge, being a form of representation, is, therefore, a metarepresentation—a representation of something (a thought, an experience) as a thought or an experience or (more specifically) a thought about this or an experience of that. If E is an experience (sensory representation) of blue, then introspective knowledge of this experience is a conceptual representation[8] of it as an experience of blue (or of color).

If, then, introspective knowledge is a species of displaced perception, it is an instance in which an experience (of blue, say) is conceptually represented as an experience of blue via a sensory representation not of the experience, but of some other object. One comes to know (the fact) that one is experiencing blue by experiencing, not the experience of blue, but some displaced object. As we shall see, this displaced object is (typically) the object the experience of blue is an experience of—i.e., the blue object one sees. Introspective knowledge of E requires no other sensory representation of objects than those already being represented by E—the experience one comes to know about.

2   Knowing Another's Mind

If introspection is direct knowledge of one's own mind, and we restrict attention to sensory affairs, introspective knowledge is direct knowledge of facts about phenomenal appearances. Since we are conceiving of how things look, feel, sound, and smell as modes of sensory representation—as the way objects (if there are any) are systemically represented—knowledge of sense experience is knowledge of how things are being represented$_s$ by the person in whom they are represented$_s$.

Before trying to answer questions about how one can know one's own mind, it will help if we begin by asking how one might know the corresponding facts about another mind. Let me start with an even simpler question. Since the topic (given the thesis I am defending) is the epistemology of representation, we can gain some leverage by asking how one might figure out how instruments represent the objects they represent. If an ordinary measuring instrument represents the F (speed, temperature, pressure, weight) of k, how would one go about finding out what it currently "says" about the F of k, what it currently represents the F of k as. If the instrument performs its indicating chores by means of a pointer, and this pointer presently occupies position P, how does one find out what position P says or means about F?

I hope this question sounds childishly simple. For if it does, then my answer, or so I hope, will also appear childishly obvious.

It is important to notice that the question is not how one might come to know what objects an instrument represents or, indeed, whether it represents an object at all. As we have already seen (chapter 1, §4), that S represents k is a hybrid representational fact. That there is an object whose pressure, speed, or curvature S represents is not itself a representational fact about S. To say that S represents k is to say both that (1) k stands in the C relation to S, and (2) for some F, S represents the F of whatever objects satisfy (1). (1), however, is not a representational fact—not, therefore, a mental—fact. To know the "mind" of an instrument is to know (2) but not (1). If instruments could introspect, if they could know their own representational states, we would expect them to know how they represent what (if anything) they represent, what determinate value of F they represent it as having, but not what object—or that there is an object—that they represent in this way. S represents what it has the function of indicating, and representational systems do not have the function of indicating what object—or that there is an object—they represent as so-and-so. If an F-representational system knows there is an object it is representing to be F, it will not know it *by introspection*. Since we are interested in introspective knowledge, we can set this kind of knowledge to one side.

How, then, would we find out how an instrument represents the objects (if any) it represents? How would we find out the representational facts, the facts that define what was going on in the representational "mind" of an instrument? To be concrete, suppose the question is a question about a particular pressure gauge. How is it representing the pressure of the tank to which it is connected. *As* what?[9]

It might seem that the answer to this question is simple: just look. The face of the gauge is, after all, marked off in pounds/square inch (psi), and the pointer is pointing at the number "14." The gauge is, therefore, representing whatever it is connected to as having a pressure of 14 psi. Even if it is not connected to anything, it certainly is representing (i.e., misrepresenting) something to be 14 psi.[10] That , after all, is what the pointer pointing at "14 psi" *means*.

This is a way of finding out what the gauge is saying, but it is a method that depends on our trusting someone to tell us what pointer positions are supposed to indicate.

Manufacturers do this (by printing numbers on the face), but this is not a courtesy that nature extends to us in the case of natural systems of representation. There are no convenient numbers in the brain—nothing to tell curious neurobiologists what (if anything) the electrical and chemical activity in there means. So, in order to impart some realism to our investigation, to make it more like the question we actually face in asking about the representational states of living systems, let us suppose there are no explanatory or interpretive symbols on the gauge. There is nothing there (or the numbers are no longer legible) to tell a curious onlooker what the pointer positions mean. We have to find this out for ourselves. I will assume that the gauge has a function, that it is, in fact, a pressure gauge,[11] and that, therefore, the various pointer positions represent$_s$ pressure. The pointer is presently occupying position P. Our question is: what does P mean, what does it represent the pressure as? Until we know this, we will not know how the instrument is "experiencing" the world, what is going on in its representational "mind."

It should be obvious that the way to answer this question is not to look more carefully at pointer position P. *That* isn't going to tell you what pointer position P means. The pointer occupying position P is the representation, of course, but you cannot find out what it "says" about pressure by looking at it. Information about how a representation of k represents k is never available in, on, or around the representation of k.[12] If this gauge "wanted" to find out how it was representing the pressure in k, it would do it no good to "peer" inwardly at its own representation of the pressure. Even if it could somehow "feel" where its pointer is pointing, this would not tell the gauge what it needs to know to know how it is representing k.

The idea that introspective knowledge is achieved by some Lockean "inner sense," a looking ("spicere") inward ("intra") at internal representations, is, I suspect, a misunderstanding of this fundamental point. The representations are inside, yes, but perceiving them will not tell you what you need to know to reach knowledge of the mind. External observers are often better positioned to observe a system's internal representations than is the system itself. We can see the instrument's pointer positions. It cannot. This, though, does not tell us what we want to know. Neither would it tell the instrument.

According to the Representational Thesis, what we have to find out about the gauge's current pointer reading is what information P is supposed to carry about pressure, what information P has the function$_s$ of providing. That will tell us what P represents$_s$ the pressure to be. Once we know what P says about pressure, we will know what the system itself, if it could introspect, would have to know if it was to know how it is representing things. How, then, does one go about determining what P means?

If we knew the instrument was working properly (as it was designed to work) and knew it was connected in the right way (i.e., by C) to k, then there would be a straightforward way of telling what P means. One would simply determine, by independent means, what the pressure in k is when the gauge is in state P. *That* would be what P means. To find out what P means about pressure, find out what pressure it has the function of indicating. To find out what pressure it has the function of indicating, find out what the pressure is when the gauge is in state P and functioning the way it is supposed to function. If the pressure is 14 psi, then, if the gauge is doing what it has the function of doing, then the state it occupies must have the function of indicating 14 psi. That, then, will be what P *means*.

The reasoning goes like this: If you have a system whose function it is to indicate F, then, if it is functioning properly (perceiving veridically, as it were), then things will "appear" to it the way things really are. The states it occupies will mean whatever the actual value of F is. So assign meanings to the states by determining what the actual values of F are when the system is working right. This is, in effect, a calibrational process—a process in which one determines what states mean by comparing what the system says, when it speaks truly, with the facts about which it speaks.[13]

But how does one tell that a system is functioning properly and is being used in the kind of circumstances, and with the kind of objects, for which it was designed? In the case of artifacts, of course, there is no special problem. Such devices come with instruction manuals and carefully calibrated scales that tell the user what the pointer positions mean. Even when no one tells us what P means (or we can't interpret the symbols), we can (knowing something about such devices and the commercial intentions with which they are made) make reasonable conjectures about how the instrument is supposed to be used, how it is to be connected, and whether it is performing well. We can, therefore, make reasonable inferences about what its various pointer readings mean by seeing what the pressure is when the instrument is (we conjecture) working properly. In the case of natural systems (the sense organs in animals), we have some information—how much depending on the animal and the sense organ in question—about when these systems are functioning in the way they were (we conjecture) designed (by natural selection) to function. There is, of course, no guarantee that we will get it right. Perhaps the indicator function of a system, the kind of information it was "designed" (by natural selection) to provide, is not what we think it is. But the same can be said about any bodily organ to which we attribute a function. We might be wrong about what its function is. The evolutionary history may not have been what we think it was. But if there is no special problem about telling whether hearts, kidneys, and pituitary glands are functioning properly, there should be no special problem in finding out whether visual or auditory systems are functioning properly. There are, to be sure, *practical* problems about figuring out what anything is for. We cannot go back in time to observe the selectional processes that, in the case of the senses, gave these systems their indicator functions$_s$. Even if we could, we would still have the problem of determining *which* of the many kinds of information a system supplied was the kind or kinds it was selected to provide—the one(s), therefore, it has the function of supplying. That is a question about which of a system's traits (in this case, indicator properties) were the ones causally responsible for its selection.

So what an external observer needs to know to determine how a system (whether natural or artifactual) is representing an object is what its reaction to that object *means*, and what the reaction of a system means is what value of F the reaction is a reaction to when the instrument is functioning the way it was designed to function. Given that the system has the function of indicating what value F is, and given that the system is in state P, what would the value of F be if the system was working right? If a system's reaction to k is P, and, when it is functioning properly, P is the system's way of reacting to a pressure of 10 psi, then the system is representing k as having a pressure of 10 psi. If it turns out that the pressure in k is actually 14 psi, then the system, in occupying state P, misrepresents the pressure in k. Putting the gauge in proper working order, and connecting it to a tank at 10 psi, is the way we tell that P means 10 psi, but the gauge doesn't have to be in proper working order for P to mean 10 psi. It means that even when things go wrong.

3   Knowing One's Own Mind

If this is the way external observers go about determining how a device—natural or artificial—is representing the objects it represents, how would the device itself go about finding this out? By means of occupying a certain state P, our gauge represents the pressure in k as 14 psi. How might the gauge come to know what P represents the pressure in k as?

It might seem as though the gauge has to do what external observers have to do. It has to go through the elaborate process described in §2. Since this is the way *we* find out what P means, this, it might be thought, is the way the gauge would have to find it out.

But is this possible? The gauge, surely, is not equipped to tell that it is in proper working order. And even if it was, how might it gain access to pressures that are known, on independent grounds, for the purpose of calibrating its own responses to pressure? If the system has access, on independent grounds, to the pressure, then we are no longer talking about a simple pressure gauge. We are talking, minimally, about two instruments—one of which is used to calibrate the other. This being so, we are no longer talking about a representational system knowing how *it* represents the world, but how one part of a composite representational system knows how the other part represents the world. This, though, puts us right back into the situation of an external observer—one system knowing, by an elaborate calibrational process—and, thus, indirectly and inferentially—how another represents the world. If this is what it takes for a representational system to know how it represents the world, then it seems to be impossible for a representational system to know, in a direct and unmediated way, representational facts about itself.

This reasoning overlooks a crucial asymmetry. When I, an external observer, try to determine what state P means in system S, I do not, whereas S does, occupy the state whose representational content is under investigation. S, therefore, *has* information—whatever information is carried by state P—that I do not. Information (about what P represents *k* as) that an external observer can only obtain by an elaborate calibrational procedure is information that S itself obtains by merely representing *k*. For in representing *k* as, say, 14 psi, S automatically—and necessarily—has absolutely reliable information about what the pressure in *k* would be if S was working right. In representing *k* as 14 psi S occupies a state (viz., P) that is perfectly correlated with (hence, carries information about) what *k* would be (i.e., 14 psi) if P were functioning properly. Thus, although P may not carry information about *k,* it does carry information about S—about the way S is representing *k.*

That is the difference between the representational system itself and external observers (you and me) trying to find out how it is representing the world. The system itself necessarily occupies a state that carries information about what the world would be like if the system was functioning properly. You and I do not. That is why we must go through the elaborate process described above. When I try to find out what the gauge is representing *k* as, I have to look at both the gauge and the world—at the gauge to tell that it is working right, and the world (i.e., *k*) to find out what the world *is* like when the gauge is in state P. These two sources of information tell me what the informational function of the state P is, what the world is like when the gauge (in state P) is doing its job. But the instrument itself, in occupying P, need only look at the world, at whatever it is already "looking" at (i.e., k) to get this information. P (the state the instrument gets itself into by "looking at" k) is a state that represents the world and carries information about itself. This result—a result of thinking about perception in representational terms—is precisely what is needed to make self-knowledge an instance of displaced perception—a process whereby a system gets information about itself (sufficient for knowing facts about itself) by perceiving, not itself, but something else. On a representational theory of the mind, this is the source of first-person authority.

This does not mean that every representational systems has self knowledge. Gauges do not. Animals do not. Infants do not. And, for most of the representational states they occupy, most adults do not. All we have so far shown is that every representational system, in representing the world, has all the information it needs to know how it is representing the world. But something more than information is needed to know. Otherwise simple instruments (which provide information to us) would end up knowing things. What more is needed is belief, the power of metarepresentation, the power to represent oneself, or some of one's internal states, as representing the pressure to be 14 psi. This is something that not every—in fact, not many—representational systems have. The final section is devoted to this particular aspect of introspective knowledge.

Before we take up this matter, though, a word should be said about exactly what information is available to a system that has representational powers. This is especially important because it bears on a paradoxical aspect (mentioned earlier) of externalist theories of the mind—the fact that first person authority seems jeopardized by conceiving of the facts (i.e., mental facts) that are known introspectively as facts constituted by relations (including—on the present account of things—historical relations) existing between what is in the head and what is not. I shall come back to these issues in chapter 5 where I consider a variety of objections to externalist theories of the mind—in particular, representational theories—but something should here be said about exactly what information (about its own representational states) I take to be available to a representational system and, thus, what is knowable by introspective means.

Tyler Burge (1988) and John Heil (1988, 1992) argue that externalism about the mind—at least externalism of the right sort—does *not* threaten first-person authority.[14] The present chapter is my way of saying why I agree with them. If one understands that introspection is a process in which information about *internal* affairs is gained in the act of representing (perceiving) *external* objects, the fact that what one learns (introspectively) about oneself are extrinsically constituted facts is no longer a problem. The extrinsicness of the mind is only a problem if one thinks one comes to know these extrinsic facts by looking inward, at the experiences these facts are facts about. That would be paradoxical.

Nonetheless, though I agree with them that an externalist theory of mental content is no bar to direct and authoritative self-knowledge of what that content is (of what it is one thinks and experiences), an externalist theory does create genuine obstacles to self-knowledge. The problem, however, isn't in knowing *what* you believe and experience. The problem is in knowing *that* you believe and experience it. The problem centers not on the content, but on the attitude (the relation) one has to that content. Let me explain.

I am (let us suppose) very expert at identifying cars. I am the world's leading authority. If you want to know what kind of car Clyde owns, just show me the car. I'll tell you. I know Clyde owns a Buick, Tom a BMW, and Carol a Dodge. But, if truth be known, I am not very good about facts pertaining to ownership. The legal niceties are beyond me. Is it the bank or Clyde that owns the car? I don't know. When someone buys a car, just when does ownership transfer? I don't know. Ask someone else. I'll tell you whether it is a Buick that Clyde owns, but ask someone else whether he owns it. If people own the cars they drive, I know what car they own, but, if push comes to shove, not that they own it. Likewise, we are all very good—in fact, absolute authorities—about what we think and experience, but not very good (in fact, I think, very bad) about the attitudinal aspect of these mental states. Both Burge and Heil argue that higher-order belief about (lower-order) thought (and, presumably, experience) has a reflexive character. In self-ascribing a belief to ourselves (as we do in higher-order belief that we believe P) the higher-order belief (= metarepresentation) attributes to the lower-order representation exactly the same content (i.e., P) that the lower-order representation carries. If this is how it works, then, even if externalism about content is true, you really can't be wrong in believing that it is P you believe since what you believe you believe is borrowed, so to speak, from what you believe. If it really is P that you (first-order) believe, then it has to be true that it is P you (second-order) believe yourself to believe since the second-order belief attributes to the first-order belief whatever content it, in fact, has. So you really cannot go wrong in identifying the content of the lower-order belief.

But just as knowing that it is a Buick Clyde owns is only part of knowing that he owns a Buick (you also have to know he owns it), knowing it is P one believes is only *part* of knowing that one believes P. One also has to know one believes it, that one stands in those relations to P that constitute believing. In the case of self-knowledge, we get information (I have argued) about the way we experience (represent) the objects we experience (as blue, say, not red or green), but I have not argued that we get information that we stand in that relation to what it is we experience that justifies calling the resulting state an experience of blue. *If* it is an experience, it is certainly an experience of blue. *If* Clyde owns it, it is (you can take my word for it) certainly a Buick that he owns. But, in both cases, there is no authoritative information about the antecedent. Burge and Heil do not argue that, in the case of higher-order belief, there is any information about whether the lower-order state (that has P as its content) is one of belief or some other attitude. Or no attitude at all. All they argue is that, if the lower-order state has content, identification of the content as P is authoritative. All they argue is that *if* you believe P, you cannot be wrong (in present-tensed self-ascriptions) about its being P you believe. They have not argued that you cannot be wrong about believing P.[15]

Nor have I. I have argued that in representing something as F a system has information about how it is representing things—as F (rather than G or H). You cannot represent something as F without, necessarily, occupying a state that carries the information that it is F (not G or H) that you are representing something as. But I have not argued that in representing something as F a system necessarily carries information that it is representing F, that it stands in those relations to the property F that constitute representation. I did not argue for this because I think it is false. Representational systems have privileged information (which is not to say they *know*—see below) about how they are representing things, but they have no information—let alone privileged information—that that is what they are doing. Representational systems have the function of supplying information about the world, not about themselves. The same is true of minds in so far as they are representational systems. What we know by introspection is not that we have a mind, but what is "in" the mind—i.e., the way things are being represented.

The situation with respect to introspective knowledge—knowledge of what is going on inside our own mind—is exactly parallel to perceptual knowledge—knowledge of what is going on outside our mind. What we see (hear, smell, etc.) is what there is in the external world, not that there is an external world. I know it is a tomato (not a banana, an apricot, or a pencil) in front of me because I can see that it is. If I want to make absolutely sure, I can feel it. But I cannot, of course, see and feel that I am not hallucinating. I cannot see or feel that my visual and tactile experiences are veridical. The senses are charged with the job of telling us what is in the external world, not the job of telling us that they are doing their job right, that there *is* an external world. If we know there is an external world, it is not by seeing or smelling.[16] Knowledge of internal affairs is no different. If we know not only what we experience and think (i.e., what exists "in" the mind), but that we experience and think it (that there is a mind it exists in), we do not know this by introspection.

What the Representational Thesis provides, then, is what it should provide. And no more. It reveals the source of first-person authority about the contents of the mind, about what it is we think and experience. It tells us how we know it is F we experience. It does not tell us how (or whether) we know we experience F, how (or whether) we know that we stand in those relations to F that make F part of the mind (i.e., a mental content). It shouldn't. That is the business of epistemology.[17]

4   Knowledge without Experience

Gauges do not introspect. Nor do animals. Or small children. They do not know things about their own representational efforts. They do not have the power to represent themselves (or anything else) as representing things in a certain way. They have representational powers (conventional and derived in the case of instruments; natural in the case of animals and small children), but they do not have metarepresentational powers.

The argument, therefore, has not been that representational systems know how they are representing the world (most of them do not), but, rather, that they necessarily have information about how they are representing the world that is more direct than that of external observers who can observe both the external affairs the system represents and the system's internal representations. The conclusion is that a system *could* know (in some privileged way), not that it does know (in any way whatsoever), facts about its own representational states, that it always—and necessarily—has information about its own representational states sufficient unto knowing what their content is. But information sufficient unto knowing facts can be available without those facts being known. What is also needed are the conceptual resources for representing the fact to be known and an appropriate "connecting belief" if the knowledge is reached by means of displaced perception. If I don't know what a postman is, the fact that the dog only barks when the postman arrives will not enable me to hear (by the dog's bark) that the postman has arrived. Displaced perception will not occur—it cannot occur—until I learn something about post-men (enough to enable me to believe that a postman has arrived) and acquire the connecting belief that the barking dog is a reliable sign (= carries the information) that the postman has arrived.

For the same reason, it is not enough for introspection, not enough to have direct knowledge of mental facts, that one have access to information about those facts. A small child (or the cat, for that matter) has access to the same information about the postman's arrival as I do. They can hear the dog barking as well as I can, and the dog's bark carries the same information (about the postman) to them that it carries to me. But neither the child nor the cat, in hearing the dog bark, knows (as I do) that the postman has arrived. They lack the right concepts, and, even if they had those concepts, they might lack the appropriate connecting beliefs needed to use the dog's bark as a means of perceiv-ing (displaced) the postman's arrival. That, basically, is the same reason they do not have introspective knowledge. They have the information, but not the understanding.[18]

Perner (1991) has nicely summarized the evidence bear-ing on a child's ability to understand representational facts and, therefore (on a representational theory), mental facts. Such an understanding, the power of metarepresentation, appears to develop between the ages of three and four years (Perner 1991, pp. 82, 189; also see Flavell 1988; Wellman 1990; Gopnik 1993). Not having a concept of representation does not prevent one from representing things, but it cer-tainly prevents one from believing (hence, knowing) that one is doing it. Until a child understands representation, it cannot conceptually represent (hence, cannot believe; hence cannot know) that anything—including itself—is representing (and, therefore, possibly misrepresenting) something as F. What prevents small children and animals from introspecting is not the lack of a mysterious power that adults have to look inward at their own representations. They already have all the information they need, and they needn't look inward to get it. What they lack is the power to give conceptual embodiment to what they are getting information about.

It may seem as though this account of introspective knowledge—as a species of displaced perception—makes it into a form of inferential, and thus indirect, knowledge. If introspective knowledge of oneself—that one represents the world thus and so—has the same structure as knowing that the postman has arrived by hearing the dog bark, then there is an intermediate "step" in the reasoning that makes knowledge of the target fact indirect. There are two ways of knowing that the postman has arrived: by seeing or hearing him arrive and by seeing or hearing something *else* (the dog) that "tells" you he has arrived. If, on a representational theory, introspective knowledge is more like the latter than the former, then the representational account fails to give self-knowledge the immediacy we know it to have.

This point is certainly relevant, but there are two important differences between introspective knowledge and other forms of displaced perception that neutralize the objection. The first point is that although I cannot hear that the mailman has arrived by hearing the dog bark unless the dog is, in fact, barking (and I hear it)—unless, that is, I truly represent the the intermediate fact that "tells" me the postman is here—I can know how I am representing some object without truly representing the intermediate "fact" that provides me with this information about myself. My representation$_s$

of k (as blue, say) does not have to be veridical for this representation to carry information about the target fact, about me, about how I am representing k. If my representation of the dog is not veridical (if I hear it as barking when it is not), my representation of the dog will not carry information about the postman. As a result, there will be no displaced knowledge. In the case of self knowledge, though, my sensory representation of the intermediate fact need not be veridical for it to carry information about me, about how I am representing things Displaced knowledge is still possible. I do not have to *truly* represent the color of k in order to get information about myself from my sensory representation of k. In the case of introspection, the perception is displaced, yes, but the necessary information is there *whether or not the intermediate representations* are veridical. If this is inferential knowledge, it is a strange case of inference: the premises do not have to be true to establish the conclusion.

Secondly, the connecting belief in the case of introspective knowledge is not defeasible. It may turn out that the dog changes its habits—it starts barking at other people. Should this happen, I can no longer come to know (though I may still be led to believe) that the postman has arrived by hearing the dog bark. The connecting belief is no longer true. But the connecting belief in the case of introspective knowledge is not, in this way, fallible. If you "see" k as blue and infer from this "fact"—the "fact" that k is blue—that you are representing k as blue, you cannot go wrong. As long as the inference is from what you "see" k to be (whether this is veridical or not) the conclusion must be true: blue must be the way you are representing k. The postman cannot fail to be there when this dog barks.[19]

Once again, if this is inferential knowledge, it is a very unusual form of inference. The premises need not be true and the inference cannot fail. As long as one's conclusion (about how one is representing things) is based on premises concerning how things are "perceived" to be, one cannot go wrong. This, I submit, is the source of the "directness" and "immediacy" of introspective knowledge.

Besides explaining first-person authority, this account of introspective knowledge explains a fact that is otherwise puzzling on "inner sense" theories of introspection. It explains why introspection has no phenomenology or, if it does, why it always has the *same* phenomenology as the experience one is introspecting. If one is asked to say what one's current visual experiences are like, for example, one seems able to know this without having any identifiable experiences other than the visual ones one is able to describe. If one is asked to introspect one's current gustatory experience—"Tell us, if you can, exactly how the wine tastes"—one finds oneself attending, not to one's experience of the wine, but to the wine itself (or perhaps the tongue or palette). There seems to be no other relevant place to direct one's attention. At least one does not have experiences other than the wine-experience one is asked to describe. If there is an inner sense, some quasi-perceptual faculty that enables one to know what experiences are like by "scanning" them, this internal scanner, unlike the other senses, has a completely transparent phenomenology. It does not "present" experiences of external objects in any guise other than the way the experiences present external objects. If one is aware of experiences in the way one is aware of external objects, the experiences look, for all the world, like external objects. This is very suspicious. It suggests that there is not really another sense in operation at all.[20]

A representational approach to the mind gives a satisfying explanation of this fact. Introspection has no phenomenology because the knowledge one gets by it is (itself) experience-less. One can, by introspection, come to know about experience, but the knowledge is obtained without any experiences beyond the ones one comes to know about. To know I am experiencing bluely, to know that that is the kind of color experience I am having, I need only the experience of blue. I don't need *another* experience. Given that I understand the concept of experience and its qualities, I have, in my experience of blue, all I need to know what kind of experience I am having. There is no need for an experience of the experience. All one needs is a belief about it.

3   Qualia

For a materialist there are no facts that are accessible to only one person. There may be circumstances of time and place that enable one person to know something others do not, circumstances of time and place that make one person authoritative, but there are no person-privileged facts, facts that only one person *can* know about. If the subjective life of another being, what it is like to be that creature, seems inaccessible, this must be because we fail to understand what we are talking about when we talk about its subjective states. If S feels some way, and its feeling some way is a material state of S, how can it be impossible for us to know how S feels?

The Representational Thesis identifies the qualities of experience—qualia—with the properties objects are represented$_s$ as having. The properties that S represents$_s$ things to have is, in principle knowable by others. Though each of us has direct information about our own experience (see chapter 2) , there is no privileged access. If you know where to look, you can get the same information I have about the character of my experiences. This is a result of thinking about the mind in naturalistic terms. Subjectivity becomes part of the objective order. For materialists, this is as it should be.

1 French Poodles and French Wine

Susan, a child of normal eyesight and intelligence, has never seen a dog. She doesn't know what dogs are. The first one she sees is a French poodle. Does it look like a poodle to her? Susan will not say or think it is (or looks like) a poodle. She will not see it *as*, or see that it is, a poodle. This is not the way she will conceptualize what she sees. Will it, nonetheless, look like a poodle to her?

Arthur is a young toad of normal toad-eyesight and toad-intelligence. He has never seen a dog. The first one he sees happens to be a poodle—the same one Susan sees. Does it look like a poodle? Like Susan, Arthur will not say or think it is (or looks like) a poodle. He will not see it as, or see that it is, a poodle. This is not the way he will conceptualize what he sees. Will it, nonetheless, look like a poodle to him?

Given what we know about the eyesight of human beings and toads, it seems clear that the poodle looks different to Susan than it does to Arthur. The dog looks to Susan the way poodles look to you and me—different from the way bulldogs, terriers, and sheepdogs look. You and I can describe the way the dog looks ("like a poodle") and Susan cannot, but this, surely, makes no difference to how the dog looks to her. Arthur is different. Though the dog looks to Arthur the way poodles look to normal toads, and Arthur is a normal toad, the dog does not look like a poodle to Arthur. Poodles do not look like poodles to half-blind people despite the fact that they look the way poodles normally look to half-blind people. Poodles look like blurry spots to half-blind people—the same almost everything else this size looks. Toads have the visual acuity of half-blind people. So poodles look to toads the way poodles look to half-blind people.

In saying that the dog looks like a poodle to Susan I am not saying that Susan's visual experience of the poodle represents it as a poodle and, therefore *mis*represents it in some way if it is not a real poodle. No, we are here speaking of sensory, not conceptual, representations of the poodle. Susan's experience of the dog represents the dog as a poodle in the sense that it represents the dog as having what McGinn (1982, p. 40; see also Millar 1991, p. 42) describes as the manifest properties of poodles, those properties that make poodles look so much different from other dogs (not to mention bicycles, etc.). A variety of nonpoodles also have the manifest properties of poodles: *trompe l'oeil*, pictures of poodles, disguised terriers, poodle robots, and so on. These objects also look like poodles. They, too, produce, poodle qualia in Susan. Although she would be making a mistake in believing (i.e., conceptually representing) a good fake to be a poodle, Susan is not misperceiving (sensuously misrepresenting) it when she visually represents a fake poodle in the same way she visually represents a real poodle. Good fakes are supposed to cause the same kind of experiences as the originals.

Some will feel it wrong to describe anything as looking like a poodle to someone who does not have the concept of a poodle. Millar (1991, p. 32), for instance, says that a person could have pumpkin experiences of exactly the same type I have when I see a pumpkin, but if that person did not have the concept of a pumpkin, did not know what a pumpkin was, it would not "seem" to that person that there was a pumpkin there. I do not want to quarrel about words. There may be a sense of "look" and other "appear" words (especially when used with a factive clause) in which Millar is right. To keep things straight I will call these uses the *doxastic* (= belief) sense of "look" ("appear," "seem," etc.) and will subscript it accordingly (Jackson [1977, p. 30], calls it the *epistemic* use of "look"). To say that a dog looks$_d$ like a poodle to S is to say that, in the absence of countervailing considerations, this is what S would take the dog to be, what S's perception of the dog would (normally) prompt S to believe (see Millar 1991, p. 19). Describing the dog as looking$_d$ like a poodle to S implies that S has the concept POODLE, understands what a poodle is, and classifies or identifies (or *would* do so in the absence of countervailing considerations) what she sees in this way. In the doxastic sense, the dog Susan sees does not look$_d$ like a poodle to her. That isn't what her perception of the dog causes her to believe.

There is, though, another sense of these words, a sense in which if the dog looks the same to Susan as it looks to me, and it looks to me like a poodle, then it must look to Susan like a poodle whether or not she understands what a poodle is, whether or not she has the concept of a poodle. Following a long tradition, I will call this the *phenomenal* sense of "look" (look$_p$). To say that the dog looks—phenomenally—like a poodle to S (= looks$_p$) is to say two things: (1) that the dog looks to S the way poodles normally look to S; and (2) the dog looks different to S from other dogs (bulldogs, terriers, etc.).[1] The second clause—call it the *discriminatory* clause—is necessary to prevent a dog looking like a poodle to a toad (or a half blind person) to whom all dogs look the same. If you are color blind, if you cannot discriminate one color from another, an object does not look$_p$ red to you simply because it looks the same as red objects normally look to you. You do not satisfy the discrimination condition. The discrimination condition is here left deliberately vague to reflect the context-sensitivity and circumstantial relativity of these judgments (*k* can look like a poodle to you in circumstances C but not in C'). Even if there is some rare breed of dog that you cannot distinguish from a French poodle, a dog might nonetheless "look$_p$ like a French poodle to you" as long as the implied set of contrasts did not include the rare breed. This is why a dog can look$_p$ like a French poodle to one even though one cannot discriminate it from a very good fake. Fake poodles are not—not normally, anyway—in the contrast-class.[2] Hence, despite the discriminatory clause, one does not have to be able to discriminate French poodles from very good fakes in order for a dog to look$_p$ to you like a French poodle.[3]

It should be noted that simply because an object looks$_p$ F to two people does not mean it looks$_p$ the same to them. It may turn out S_1 and S_2 are equally good at discriminating Fs from other objects and that a given object, k, looks to S_1 the way Fs usually look to S_1 and looks to S_2 the way Fs usually look to S_2. None of this implies that the object looks to S_1 the way it looks to S_2. Maybe it does, maybe it doesn't. The fact that a dog looks$_p$ like a poodle to Susan *and* (say) to another poodle does not mean it looks the same to them. The possibility of inverted qualia is not foreclosed by these definitions. More of this in a moment.

With these terminological stipulations, we can say that the dog looks$_p$ like a poodle to Susan but not to Arthur (it looks$_d$ like a poodle to neither, of course). A toad's visual system was not designed to discriminate the forms of middle-sized objects in the way the visual system of humans was. The proof of this lies in the inability of toads to perceptually discriminate the shapes of middle-sized objects. Just what poodles look like to a toad depends, in part, on the toad's powers of discrimination. If, as I have been assuming (on the basis of neurophysiological and behavioral data[4]) middle-sized animals that are moving (toads don't seem able to see the stationary ones) look the same to toads, then toads cannot see differences that normal human beings see, differences in form and detail that make poodles look different from bulldogs to us. A toad's visual system does not represent$_s$ poodles the way our visual system represents$_s$ them. So poodles, I infer, must look$_p$ to toads the way poodles look to us when we see them in poor light and without our glasses—pretty much the way bulldogs and terriers look.

We are also in a better position to describe certain (otherwise) puzzling situations. Suppose all red wines taste the same to me. Does this mean that the red Burgundy I am presently tasting tastes$_p$ like a red Burgundy to me? It *does*, after all, taste the way red Burgundy normally tastes to me. No, not if I cannot discriminate it from a Chianti.[5] If Burgundies taste the same to me as Chianti, chances are neither Burgundies nor Chiantis taste like Burgundy to me. In all likelihood, both taste like an ordinary red "jug" wine. Maybe not. It depends on whether I can distinguish "jug" wine from Coca-Cola. If I stand (gustatorily) to wines the way toads stand (visually) to dogs, Burgundy and Chianti are to me what poodles and bulldogs are to toads—the gustatory equivalent of blurry spots.

Application of the same criteria for telling how things "look" or "seem" to a system is evident in the way we think and talk about instruments. If a measuring instrument is not designed to discriminate between 7.00 and 7.01, if numbers beyond the decimal point are not (as they say) significant digits for it, then the instrument cannot represent anything as 7.00. Nothing can "seem" like 7.00 to an instrument that has no internal state with the function of indicating a value of between 6.99 and 7.01. This, basically, is the reason nothing can "seem" like a poodle to Arthur. Arthur's visual system does not have the requisite "resolving" power. Nothing in Arthur has the function of indicating that yonder object has *this* (a poodle) shape rather than *that* (a bulldog) shape.

Susan's visual system is a more sensitive instrument.[6] She, as it were, experiences 7.00 shapes and Arthur does not.

We must, however, be careful in using discriminatory data in making inferences about appearances$_p$—about the quality of someone's experience. Such inferences move from premises about what animals can and cannot discriminate in a given sensory mode to conclusions about how something appears$_p$ to them in that mode. That this is fallacious—at least suspicious—can be seen by considering the wine example. Even though all red wines taste the same to me, maybe they all taste$_p$ like exquisite Burgundy and not, as I was assuming, like ordinary red table wine. If this were so, then you and I might be the same in our discriminatory powers (we both embarrass ourselves at wine tasting parties) even though all wines taste different to us. All wines taste to me the way fine Burgundies taste to a connoisseur. All wines taste to you the way cheap Chianti tastes to a connoisseur. This gustatory anomaly may be hard (impossible?) to detect. Every time you, sipping an expensive Burgundy, say that the wine tastes like *that* (gesturing toward a cheap Chianti), I agree. That is exactly the way it tastes to me.

If the wine example seems far-fetched, Clark (1993, p. 167) gives a more compelling example:

If you close one eye, stare at some bright colour for 30 seconds, and then blink your eyes successively, you will note shifts in the chromatic appearance of most things. The adaptation difference between the two eyes vanishes quickly, so the effects will soon disappear. While they last, however, these adaptation effects are similar in several ways to the purported differences between people. Discriminations made with the adapted eye will match those made with the unadapted eye. Any two items that present different hues to the unadapted eye will present different hues to the adapted eye. Matching items will continue to match as well. But the apparent hue of everything shifts.

Clark concludes by saying that the possibility of interpersonal differences of this sort seems fatal to the project of defining sensory qualities in terms of what can be discriminated. Shoemaker (1975) makes the same point.

It seems, then, that we might be indistinguishable in our discriminatory behavior and, yet, different in the way things taste to us—different in the way we sensuously represent the objects we perceive. This, of course, is the inverted spectrum problem.[7] The "problem" is a problem for those—e.g., behaviorists and functionalists[8]—who think the quality of experience must, somehow, be defined in behavioral or functional terms.

The Representational Thesis is a naturalistic theory that avoids this problem.[9] The qualitative character of perceptual experience, it concedes, is not functionally definable. It is, however, physically definable. By identifying qualia with the properties that the experience represents$_s$ things as having, a representational approach to the mind does two things: (1) It respects the widely shared (even by functionalists[10]) intuition that qualitative aspects of experience are subjective or private: they do not necessarily express themselves in the behavior (or behavioral dispositions) of the system in which they exist. (2) It provides an account of sense experience which makes the qualitative aspects of experience objectively determinable. In identifying qualia with experienced properties, experienced properties with properties represented$_s$, and the latter with those properties the senses have the natural function of providing information about, a representational approach to experience makes qualia as objectively determinable as are the biological functions of bodily organs. It may be hard—sometimes (from a practical standpoint) impossible—to discover what the function$_s$ of a certain state is, but there is nothing essentially private or exclusively first-person about functions.

Eduardo Bisiach (1992), a neuropsychologists, despairs of finding an objective way to study qualia. "There is," he says, "no way in which a natural science of consciousness could have anything to do with qualia" (p. 115). What I hope to do in the remainder of this chapter is to show that such pessimism can be avoided. A representational account of experience not only makes room for qualia, it provides an objective way of studying them.

2 Qualia as Represented Properties

It is hard to find a description of qualia with which two (let alone all) philosophers would agree, but it seems safe enough to begin by saying that the qualia in sense modality M (for S) are the ways objects phenomenally appear or seem to S in M. In accordance with the Representational Thesis, I continue to identify qualia with phenomenal properties—those properties that (according to the thesis) an object is sensuously represented (represented$_s$) as having. This means that questions about another person's (or animal's) qualia are questions about the representational$_s$ states of the person (or animal), questions about what properties these states have the function$_s$ of indicating.

As we saw in chapter 2, §2, the way an experience represents$_s$ an object is the way that object would be if the representational system were working right, the way it is supposed to work, the way it was designed to work. In the case of conventional representations, we look to the purposes and intentions of the designers and builders. If you want to know how things "seem" to a ringing doorbell, how the bell is currently representing the front door, ask what would be the case if the device was working the way it is supposed to work. *That* will be how things "seem" to the doorbell. Using this test, when the bell rings, it must "seem" to the system that there is someone at the door. That is what the ring means whether or not there is someone at the door. It does not mean that a bill collector is at the door even if, in point of fact, that is who is there. Given the operation of this system, the bell, even under optimal conditions, cannot distinguish between bill collectors and visiting relatives.[11] That is why we say that the bell means that someone is at the door—not a bill collector, not a visiting relative, but *someone*. A person hearing the bell might represent (i.e., believe) it to be a bill collector, but that is not what the bell means, not what it says or represents. The state of a representational system means whatever it has the function of indicating. That is why doorbells do not "lie" about who is at the door. They never say who is there.

Arthur's visual system cannot represent something to be a poodle for the same reason a doorbell system cannot represent someone at the door as a bill collector. The reason it cannot "seem" to a doorbell that a bill collector is at the door is the reason it cannot seem to Arthur as though there is a poodle nearby. This is not—I emphasize, *not*—because Arthur cannot distinguish poodles from bulldogs. For we can imagine Susan's eyesight so bad that she, too, cannot distinguish one from the other. Yet, though Susan could not, thus impaired, distinguish poodles from bulldogs, we can still imagine her having poodle qualia. We can imagine Susan dreaming of poodles.[12] We can imagine her hallucinating poodles. We can even imagine Susan, with vision so impaired she cannot distinguish poodles from bulldogs, hallucinating poodles when she looks at dogs—thus having poodle qualia when she sees poodles. This is what the wine example shows. We can imagine someone with virtually no ability to discriminate wines experiencing an exquisite

Burgundy taste when he or she drinks wine—any wine. Another person always experiences the taste of cheap Chianti. No, the key difference between Susan and Arthur is not the difference in their discriminatory powers. We can imagine their discriminatory powers being the same and, yet, their having quite different experiences. The key difference is not in what information their visual system provides (this might be the same), but in what information their visual systems have the function of providing.[13] Susan occupies perceptual states that, whether or not they can any longer perform their function, whether or not they enable her to distinguish poodles from bulldogs, nonetheless have the function (i.e., the function$_s$) of distinguishing middle-sized objects (like poodles and bulldogs) from one another. Arthur occupies no such state. That is why he can no more experience poodles as poodles than standard issue doorbells can represent bill collectors as bill collectors.

Imagine two instruments, J and K. J is a precision device manufactured to measure speed in hundredths of miles per hour. When it registers 78.00, that (as the digits after the decimal point suggest) means not 77.99 (and below) and not 78.01 (and above). J has a discriminating speed "palate." Instrument K is a less expensive device, designed to provide rough information about speeds. Its registration of 78 means not 77 (and below) and not 79 (and above).[14] There is no state of K (as there is of J) that has (by design) the job of indicating that the speed is between 77.99 and 78.01 speeds. Since no state has this function, no state of K represents the speed as being 78.00. K's speed "palate" is much less discriminating than J. J is a speed connoisseur. He can tell a 77.92 speed from a 77.98 speed. All these speeds "feel" the same to K. J has speed "quale" that K never "experiences."

J is the instrumental analog of Susan, K of Arthur. In representing the speed as 78.00 mph and 78 mph respectively, J and K are responding to the same objective condition just as both Susan and Arthur are responding to the same poodle. But Susan represents this object in a more discriminating way. Small changes in shape make a difference to Susan. Just as J's registration would change (from "78.00" to "78.05") if the speed changed from 78.00 to 78.05, Susan's representational "needle" would move if the objective shape changed from that of a poodle to that of a bulldog. Just as J's mechanism is sensitive to, and was designed to be sensitive to, these differences in speed, Susan's visual system is sensitive to, and (we are assuming) was designed to be sensitive to, these differences in shape. This is not true of K and Arthur. Neither of them would register, nothing in them was designed to register, these differences. Arthur represents poodles the same way he represents bulldogs—as a blob—just as K represents a speed of 78.00 the same way it represents a speed of 78.05—as 78.

We can imagine our two instruments "experiencing different qualia" (i.e., representing speed differently) while being indistinguishable in discriminatory behavior and capacity. Suppose speedometer J, via damage or wear, loses sensitivity. It becomes as insensitive to speed as K. Speeds that, before damage, "seemed" (i.e., were represented as) different to J now seem the same. After damage to J's information delivery systems, the two instruments provide the same information about speed. As the speed varies between 77.84 and 78.23 J's needle (just like K's needle) doesn't budge (it may help to think of these as digital devices). When the speed rises from 77 to 78, J (like K) sluggishly responds with a shift from "77.00" to "78.00" at approximately 77.50. The two instruments thus become functionally indistinguishable. Despite this equivalence, a registration of "78.00" on J means something different from a registration of "78" on K. The fact that J no longer delivers the information it is its function to provide does not mean that it loses the function of providing it. As long as it retains this function, a registration of "78.00" on J means something different from a registration of "78" on K even if the two responses carry the same information. After damage (injury, old age, whatever) things still "seem" like 78.00 mph to J. That is what a reading of "78.00" has (and retains) the function of indicating. J can no longer (veridically) "perceive" a speed of 78.00 mph, but J can still "hallucinate" or "dream" about this speed. K cannot. K never experienced 78.00 mph qualia and still doesn't. He cannot "dream" about 78.00 mph speeds. There is no state of K that has this representational content. The representational difference between J and K lies, not in what they do, not even what they can do, but in what their various states have the function of doing.

The difference between J and K is that J does, while K does not, have an internal state that was designed to indicate a speed of 78.00, an internal state that, therefore, has this function. J, therefore, can represent the speed to be 78.00 mph. K cannot. The fact that when things are not working properly the internal states of the two devices indicate the same thing does not imply that they *mean* the same thing. Damage changes what information a state carries (what it correlates with) but not what it means (what it has the function of correlating with). This is why we can imagine Susan, with impaired vision, seeing every dog as a poodle, but not Arthur. She has sensory states that mean this even if they no longer carry this information.

I agree, therefore, with Shoemaker (1991, p. 508), who agrees with Ned Block and Jerry Fodor (1972), that qualia are not functionally definable. But this does not mean that qualia are not capturable by a representational account of the present sort. For two representational devices can be equivalent in their discriminatory powers and capacities (hence, functionally equivalent) and, yet, occupy different representational states. Experiences can thus be different even though this difference can no longer "express" itself in discriminatory performance. Though this means that qualia are not functionally definable, it does not mean that they are not physically definable. They are physically definable as long as there is a description, in physical terms, of the conditions in which systems have information-carrying functions. As long as we have a naturalistic theory of indicator functions, we have a naturalistic theory of representation and, hence, qualia.

3   Points of View

Thomas Nagel (1974) said that ". . . every subjective phenomenon is essentially connected with a single point of view, and it seems inevitable that an objective, physical theory will abandon that point of view." A representational account of subjective phenomena constitutes an objective, naturalistic, theory of the mind that does not abandon the subjective point of view. It does not abandon points of view, it explains them.

If we compare two representational systems that represent the same set of determinables (speed, weight, temperature, etc.), their points of view are fixed by the objects they represent and the determinate forms of these determinable properties they represent these objects as having. Both S_1 and S_2 represent O, but S_1 represents it as blue while S_2 represents it as cyan (a shade of blue). Or both represent something to be cyan, but it turns out that they represent different objects—or different parts of the same object—to be cyan. In either case, they have a different point of view, one that is determined by the representational facts.

The radar at O'Hare (Chicago) and LaGuardia (New York) represents the location and movement of planes in their vicinity. The instruments have different points of view. They represent different objects in the world. One cannot tell, just by looking at the radar screen, that they have different points of view. The screens, after all, might look exactly the same. The difference in their point of view is determined, not by *how* they represent their part of the sky, but *which* part of the sky they represent. What gives the two radar systems a different perspective on the world is the different way they are connected to the world (a relation I earlier dubbed "C"), a connection that makes them sensitive to, and thus able to represent, different parts of the world. This difference in point of view is not, however, a representational (hence, in the case of natural systems, not a mental) fact about systems. Experiences do not differ subjectively just because they are experiences of different objects and, thus, constitute different points of view.

If we suppose that any objects necessarily occupy different places in the world—thus affording any two systems representing different objects different views (i.e., views of different places) of the world—then the difference in "view" created by the fact that different objects are being represented is a difference in what Biro (1991, 1992) calls a *fixed* point of view—a point of view that can be exchanged by changing places with each other. The O'Hare radar can be moved to LaGuardia—thus coming to have the same (fixed) point of view as the LaGuardia radar. Biro points out that there is nothing mental about fixed points of view—nothing it is "like" (in Nagel's sense) to occupy or change fixed points of view. Different points of view can be experientially the same. The O'Hare and the LaGuardia screens, although having different points of view, could be in exactly the same representational state. Differences in experiential state are not the result of differences in point of view, but of differences in the way the points are viewed. If we see different objects, but they are twins, we occupy different (fixed) points of view, but our experiences are the same. We could exchange fixed points of view without so much as a ripple in our conscious life. What makes a difference in what it is like to have an experience, in the quality of experience, is not the objects the experience is an experience of—not, therefore, our (fixed) point of view—but the way these objects are represented from that point of view.[15]

Even when F-representational systems are representing the same object they can represent it, so to speak, at different degrees of magnification or over different ranges. They can, therefore, embody differing "perceptions" of this object— the same kind of difference that we experience when we look at small print with the naked eye and through a magnifying glass. In Section §2 we saw how an instrument could provide a "close up" view of the same magnitude. One speedometer represents the speed as 78.00 mph while another represents it as 78 mph. The first has a "close up" view that changes with small perturbations in the speed. To a sensitive instrument a speed of 78.05 "looks different" from a speed of 78.00. To a less sensitive instrument these speeds "look" the same. Hence, even if these instruments are veridically "perceiving" (representing) the same object, they see it differently. One has better vision or it is, so to speak, "standing closer." It has a "better view" of the object. Such differences in points of view help to define *what it is like* to have that point of view, but they are easily captured within a representational idiom.

4   What Is It Like to Experience Electric Fields?

There is an argument due to Frank Jackson (1986) that if you do not experience color (hue) for yourself, then a certain piece of factual knowledge remains inaccessible to you. You do not know what it is like to experience red, blue, and other colors. The argument easily generalizes. How can someone without a sense of smell know what lilacs or burning toast smells like? There are, it seems, facts you cannot know without having had certain experiences. But if this is so, then some knowledge, knowledge of what those experiences are like, is reserved for those who experience them. This, in turn, makes it seem as though there are aspects of subjectivity—what it is like to experience F—that are inaccessible to objective determination. If you have to experience F to know what it is like to experience F, then, if there is any reason to think (as there is) that other people—certainly other animals—experience things you do not, then there is reason to think there are facts you cannot know about the experience of others.

This version of The Problem of Other Minds strikes many people as being persuasive. It also suggests that the hope for an objective study, a *science*, of the mind—at least that part of the mind given over to subjective experience—is a will-o'-the-wisp. How can we know what a neighbor's experience is like—not to mention the experience of aliens and animals—unless we can somehow get into their heads and experience what they are experiencing?

The Representational Thesis reveals what is wrong with this reasoning. Knowing what bats, fish, and neighbors experience is, in principle, no different from knowing how things "seem" to a measuring instrument. In both cases it is a question of determining how a system is representing the world. Though this is difficult—sometimes, from a practical standpoint, impossible—it does not require the conceptual impossibility of getting "inside" the head of another being.

I borrow Jackson's protagonist, Mary, to illustrate the point. Mary is an expert on electromagnetic phenomena. She understands all about magnetic and electric fields, Maxwell's equations, quantum electrodynamics, and so on. But she has never experienced an electric field. She has heard that sharks and dogfish have an electromagnetic sense that enables them to detect prey by sensing distortions (often created by prey) in the earth's electric field. What, she wonders, would it like to be a dogfish and experience electric fields?

Mary is not asking to *be* a dogfish. In wanting to know what it is like to be a dogfish, all Mary wants to know is how things seem to dogfish when they, via their electromagnetic sense, detect prey. What sort of qualia are produced by a sensory system that detects deformations in electric fields?

Since dogfish are fairly complicated animals, it will help if we begin with something simpler—a mono-representational parasite.[16] I return to dogfish in a moment.[17] Imagine, then, our parasite attaching itself to hosts when, and only when, the host is at a certain temperature: 18°C. Since the temperature of the host is critical to the survival of the parasite, it has evolved an acute thermal sense. It is capable of registering the temperature within fractions of a degree of bodies with which it comes in contact.[18] The parasite senses a potential host as being 18°C—the ideal temperature—and attaches itself. The host does not have to *be* 18°C. All that is necessary to bring about attachment to the host is that the parasite sense it as, represent it to be, 18°C. The question is: what is it like to be this parasite when it senses a receptive host?

If you know what it is to be 18°C, you know how the host "feels" to the parasite. You know what the parasite's experience is like as it "senses" the host. If knowing what it is like to be such a parasite is knowing how things seem to it, how it represents the objects it perceives, you do not have to be a parasite to know what it is like to be one. All you have to know is what temperature is. If you know enough to know what it is to be at a temperature of 18°C, you know all there is to know about the quality of the parasite's experience. To know what it is like for this parasite, one looks, not in the parasite, but at what the parasite is "looking" at—the host. For, if things are working right, what the host is—18°C—is how things seem to the parasite. So if you want to know how things seem to the parasite, look at the host.

This will surely sound preposterous to some.[19] Surely knowing what temperature is will not tell one what it is like (if it is like anything) for a parasite (or even another human being) to *feel* a temperature of this kind. Deaf people can know what sound waves are without knowing what it is like to *hear* sound waves. I do not wish to deny this. I am *not* denying it. I will, in the remainder of this section, and especially in the next section, try to say more fully *why* I am not denying it. For the moment, though, I beg the reader's indulgence. I am merely drawing out the consequences of facts that almost everyone accepts—facts that are quite independent of the representational point of view being defended in these lectures. The first fact is that qualia are supposed to be the way things seem or appear in the sense modality in question. So, for example, if a tomato looks red and round to S, then redness and roundness are the qualia of S's visual experience of the tomato. If this is so, then (second fact) if things ever *are* the way they seem, it follows that qualia, the properties that define what it is like to have that experience, are exactly the properties the object being perceived *has* when the perception is veridical. Since in the case of our parasite, the property the object (the host) has when the perception is veridical is the property of being 18°C, that has to be the quale of the parasite's experience of the host whether or not the parasite is perceiving the host veridically (whether or not the host actually has this property). So anyone who knows what 18°C is, knows what this property is, knows what quale the parasite's experience has. They know, with respect to this single quale, what it is like to be that parasite. If that result is absurd, then one of the two facts that led to it—not the Representational Thesis—is to blame.

Back to dogfish. Mary knows all about electric fields and irregularities in electric fields. She knows everything there is to know about electric fields in the way you know everything there is to know (there isn't much) about moving at a speed of 4 mph. If the dogfish's electromagnetic sense is functioning normally, then it is representing patterns in the electric field. The field is normal here, it is "pinched in" there, and it "bulges" between here and there. There is, then, an irregularity in the field whose geometry is describable. We can describe the configuration of the field. I just did. Mary, who knows all about electric fields and how fish, rocks, and plants deform them, could draw an exact picture of the field. What she draws (describes, represents, or knows) about the electric field is what the fish senses about the electric field in which it finds itself. In drawing, describing, representing, and knowing the geometry of the field, Mary draws, describes, represents, and knows what it is like to be a dogfish (veridically) sensing that kind of field. Just as you—knowing what it is like to have four sides—know what it is like to *look* (phenomenally) four-sided,[20] Mary, in knowing what the shape of the field is, knows what an experience of a field of this shape is like. In knowing what an experience of a field of this shape is like, Mary knows, with respect to this single dimension of the experience, what it is like to have an experience of this sort. She knows this quale of the dogfish's experience. There is nothing more to know about how an electric field of that shape seems to the dogfish. On almost any theory of experience—certainly on a representational theory—there is no more to the quality of one's experiences in experiencing blue than there is to the color blue since the color blue *is* the color one experiences. It is the quality that distinguishes one's blue experiences from other color experiences. Likewise, there is no more to experiencing an electric field of type T than there is to being an electric field of type T since T is exactly what makes this electric field experience different from other experiences of the electric field. T is the quale of this experience. If Mary knows what a field of type T is, she knows all there is to know about the quality of experiences of this type.

To know what the quality of an experience is is not necessarily to be able to recognize something as having that quality when you experience it yourself. I know enough musical theory to know what a change of key is. If I know that you hear a change of key, I know exactly what your experience is like in this single respect. Your experience has that change-of-key-quality, and I know what this quality is. Nonetheless, despite knowing this fact about your experience, I do not myself have the skill or ability to recognize a change of key when I hear it myself. As Lewis (1983), Nemirow (1980), and others have pointed out, there is an ability sense of knowing-what-it-is-like that I need not possess to know what it is like (in the fact sense) to hear a change of key. If I know what a change of key is, then, in the fact sense, I know what it is like to hear a change of key. It is like *that* where the "that" refers to what I know to be a change of key. This does not mean I could tell, by hearing, that something is *that*. That is an ability that is not required to know what quality your experience has when it has the change-of-key-quality. And the same is true of Mary. Knowing the quality of a dog-fish's experience does not require Mary to be able to identi-fy, via any sense modality, what the dogfish identifies by its electric sense.

It is important to understand that the dogfish is not being said to represent the electric field as an electric field—much less an electric field of such-and-such form. The fact that it is an electric field that has this shape is not what is being rep-resented. What the fish represents about the electric field is its configuration, its geometry, its shape. The theoretical constitution of whatever it is that has that shape is another matter. If we suppose that the temperature of a gas is the energy of the gas's molecules, then in representing the tem-perature of a gas to be 78° a thermometer represents the molecules to have an energy of 78°. But in representing the molecules to have an energy of 78°, the thermometer does not represent the gas as having molecular constituents— much less as having molecular constituents with an energy of 78°. Thermometers represent the energy of the molecular constituents as being 78° (rather than 77° or 79°), not as being the energy of molecular constituents. In order to eat, dogfish have to know about the configuration of the electric field. They do not have to know that it is an electric field that has this configuration. The same is true of Mary. In order to know how the fish represent the field, she has to know what shape they represent it to be. She does not have to know what representing something as an electric field might be like. She does not because dogfish do not represent$_s$ electric fields as electric fields. Why should they?

So, in running discrimination tests on dogfish, Mary is determining just which deformations of the electric field the dogfish is sensitive to and which it is "blind" to. Mary is thereby learning exactly what it is like (for dogfish) to sense electric fields. In charting the discriminatory powers of the dogfish with respect to electric fields (assuming the electrical sense of these fish has the function of informing them of the shape of this field), Mary is determining the character of the fish's perceptual experience, how their experience represents the electrical environment. Once this is known—and there is nothing preventing Mary from knowing all of it—there is nothing more to know about the dogfish's awareness of electric fields.[21]

There is one thing dogfish can do that Mary cannot do. Suppose a fish experience an electric field of pattern P. If these fish could think, this fish could think that *this* (referring to an experienced electric field) has pattern P. Mary cannot. Not being aware of any electric field, Mary knows nothing that can be expressed in quite this form. For Mary there is no object she is aware of (a *this*) that is an electric field of pattern P. Knowing what she does about electric fields, May knows exactly what the fish is experiencing, exactly what the fish is referring to with its demonstrative "this" and what shape the fish is experiencing it to have. Nonetheless, Mary cannot herself describe what she knows the fish experiences in the way the fish experiences it. But this, surely, does not show that the dogfish experiences something that Mary doesn't know about. You and I both know my keys are on the table, but only I can express what we both know with the words: "My keys are on the table."

You have to use different words to refer to what you know to be on the table (what it is you know I know)—e.g., "*Your* keys are on the table." The fact that we cannot refer to what we know to be on the table in the same way does not mean that there is something different we know. And the fact that Mary doesn't stand to the electric field in the relation that allows her to refer to it in the way the dogfish experiences it (as a *this*) does not show there is something about the dog-fish's experience that Mary does not know.

What I am experiencing when I experience blue is some-thing I can describe by saying, "This is the color blue." You might know I am experiencing blue—thus know exactly what I know—yet, because you are differently situated, not be able to express what you know in the way I do. There is nothing you can refer to as *this* that is the color quality I happen to be experiencing. This does not show you do not know what the quality of my experience is. And the fact that Mary cannot experience electric fields does not show she cannot know exactly what dogfish experiences are like.[22]

I have been assuming throughout this discussion that there was no particular problem about the determinable being represented, only a question about which determinate form of that determinable the system represented at a given time. This assumption conceals an important problem. The problem has proved particularly vexing in the case of color (and other so-called secondary property) perception. What property is my experience of red an experience (representa-tion) of? *Red*, yes, but what objective property is this? If color qualia are identified with the properties that color experiences represent$_s$, and experiences represent$_s$ the objec-tive properties they have the function$_s$ of indicating, what objective property do experiences of color have the function$_s$ of indicating? Is it wavelength of the incident (on the retina) light? Is it a more global property of the entire optic array (see Land 1977)? Is it, perhaps, some surface property (reflectance?) of the objects that reflect light to the eye? The difficulty in finding a plausible objective property that the visual system is responding to in the case of color has led many philosophers (Hardin [1986] being a recent one) to subjectivism about color. Subjectivists do not think that colors are objective properties—thus, not objective properties that vision has the function of informing about. Even under ideal conditions, there are no objective conditions our experiences of color inform us about. Depending on conditions, light of different wavelengths will arouse the same color experience. Therefore the color experience does not "tell" us the wavelength. There is no particular spectral reflectance a surface must have to be seen as green. Depending on illumination, a host of different surface qualities can give rise to the same color experience. This general phenomenon—the fact that a wide (infinite, in fact) set of objective circumstances can give rise to the same color experience—is called metameric matching. If, then, the function of color vision is to indicate color, and color is identified with some objective property of objects (e.g., surface spectral reflectance), then either color vision in humans is doing a strikingly bad job or colors are complex disjunctions of objective conditions—all those that give rise to the same color experience. If this is so, we are left with the question of why a system (like vision) should have been selected to indicate the presence of *this* highly disjunctive (and altogether motley) collection of distal conditions? Isn't the truth of the matter that the only thing that holds together, in one class, all the diverse objects we designate as red is the fact that they all give rise to the same sort of color experience— the experience of redness? But if this is so, then we cannot define the quale red in terms of some objective property an experience has the function$_s$ of indicating (thus representing$_s$). For we are specifying the objective condition (the highly disjunctive set of surface spectral reflectances) the experience has the function$_s$ of indicating by means of the subjective qualia (experiences of redness) these objective conditions produce.

This is a complex issue and I cannot hope to do justice to it in the space of a few pages.[23] But, once again, an analogy with a conventional system may help to indicate the proper response to this problem. Earlier (chapter 1, §3) I described an instrument—a speedometer—that used information about the rate at which the axle rotates to provide information about speed. Such a device is cheaper to manufacture than an instrument that (by taking into account elevation of the axle above the road surface) automatically compensates for tire size. Since it is cheaper to manufacture, and every car in which the device is to be installed normally comes equipped with standard-size tires, there is no need to go to additional expense. The designers selected the cheaper mechanism for installation in cars because it did the job well *enough*—well enough to justify its selection over a device that was more versatile and reliable but substantially more expensive. On any rational selection procedure, this mechanism (rather than the more sophisticated one) would be chosen for the job. Given that it was selected for this job, the representational states of this device (pointer positions) thereby have the systemic function of indicating speed, not axle rotation, even though the system uses information about axle rotation to do its job.

Once we have a vehicle equipped with such a device, we have a speed-analog of metameric matching. There are a variety (infinite, in fact) number of different speeds that can give rise to a representation of 78 mph: a speed of 78 mph with normal tires, a speed of 62 mph with small tires, a speed of 93 mph with large tires, etc. If people start using tires of different sizes, then this device will no longer be able to do what it is its function to do—indicate speed. It was selected to do a certain job because it did that job—indicated speed—in a certain specified set of conditions (normal-size tires). The fact that it cannot do that job in other conditions does not mean it does not have that function$_s$ of indicating speed. All it means is that to determine what a system's function$_s$ is one has to sometimes determine the conditions in which it was selected to do it. For what it was selected to do—what it therefore has the function of doing—what it therefore represents—depends on the (possibly) special conditions existing at the time at which selection occurred.

In the case of instruments, we (designers and users) determine which of the quantities on which the instrument's behavior depends are the ones it represents. We give the instrument its function. We say that it is a speedometer. We could make the same device into an AXLE-RPM METER by giving it that job. If we gave it that job, tire size would be irrelevant to performance of its function, irrelevant to the accuracy of its representations. But we didn't do that. We are interested, primarily, in vehicle speed, not (except as an indicator of speed) axle rotation. So the instrument is given a job to do—indicate car speed—that makes it "hostage" to circumstances. It is hostage to these circumstances in the sense that unless these circumstances are right, the system will not be able to do its job even though it performs as well as it can perform. By giving our axle-rpm indicator the function of indicating vehicle-mph, we increase the number of ways it can go wrong without malfunctioning. We increase the number of what Matthen (1988) called "normal misperceptions." We enlarge the number and variety of metameric matches—the number and variety of different objective conditions that can bring about the same representational state. We, thus, increase the number of ways a system can go "wrong" while performing optimally. By extending outward—to more "distal" conditions—what the system has the function of indicating, we make it harder and harder to tell, by examining the instrument, what its representational states are. For what its states have the function of indicating depends less and less on what information the system delivers when functioning properly and more and more on the performance of that function in special circumstances.

A number of authors (Hatfield 1991, 1992; Shepard 1992) have made this same point about the relevance of actual historical conditions in evaluating the function of a system and, thus (on the present construal of representation) its representational efforts. Hatfield (1992) observes that if the function of color vision is to enhance the discriminability of, say, green plants from soil and rocks, then ". . . it would be of no consequence if there were physically possible but not actual (nonplant) metameric matches to green plants that the system could not discriminate." Judgments of function depend on what a system is designed to do, and you cannot always tell what a system is designed to do—what it thereby has the function of doing—what it, therefore, represents—by looking at what it actually does in present conditions even if you know that what it is doing is what it is supposed to be doing. It depends, in addition, on whether it is doing it in the kind of conditions that resemble the conditions in which it was selected to do that. When the speedometer described above misrepresents the speed of a car (with under-size tires) as going 62 mph, it is, in a sense, doing exactly what is designed to do, exactly what it is supposed to do. It is using information about axle rotation to tell, in accordance with a built-in algorithm, how fast the car is going. The trouble lies, not with the instrument, but with the ecology in which it is being used. These aren't the conditions in which the instrument was selected to perform.[24] The algorithm it uses to compute speed no longer applies—not with the kind of reliability for which it was selected. It would be wrong to infer that this device does not have the function of indicating a simple objective property (speed) simply because, when working properly, it responds, in exactly the same way, to an infinite variety of different speeds. This is true, but it doesn't show that it doesn't represent that infinite variety of conditions in a single way.

The same is true of color vision. If we pursue this line of thinking to its logical conclusion, we reach Hilbert's (1992, p. 362) view: that color is whatever property it is the function of color vision to detect. The fact that so many different conditions cause us to experience red does not show that what we experience when we experience red is not an objective property. It only shows that which property it is may no longer be obvious from the variety of conditions that cause us to experience it.

5   What Is It Like to Be an Experiencer of Electric Fields?

But does this really mean that we can objectively determine what it is like to be a dogfish? Or a bat? Can things really be this simple? If a bat's sonar system represents the moth as being *there*, and I understand just where (and what) there is—thereby knowing exactly where the moth seems to the bat to be—do I really understand what it is like to be a bat?

Things are not this simple, of course, but that is because we have been considering, not what it is like to be a dogfish or a bat, but what it would be like to do one of the things that dogfish and bats do—sense the geometry of electric fields or the spatial location of moths. But that is surely not all that dogfish and bats experience. Until we know everything they do by way of representing their surroundings, we will not know everything there is to know about how they experience the world. We won't, therefore, know what it is like to be a dogfish or a bat.

There is, in other words, a difference between knowing what it is like to sense F (which S does) and knowing what it is like to be an S (which senses F). To know what it is like to be S we have to know (with regard to sensory qualia) *all* the properties that S senses. In knowing exactly what configurational qualities the dogfish experiences in sensing the deformation of an electric field, Mary may still be ignorant about what else there is to the fish's phenomenal world, what other properties of its surroundings or the electric field (besides its geometry) the fish is experiencing. Does the fish not only sense the spatial layout of the field, but variations in its intensity? Is it also sensitive to induced magnetic fields? Phase relations? It would be a mistake for aliens to conclude that they knew what it was like to see objects because they knew everything there was to know about location, size, shape, and orientation—the qualia we experience (and they knew we experienced) in seeing objects. If they did not understand color and that, in seeing objects, we also represent their reflectance properties (if that is, indeed, what color is), there is an aspect of our experience of objects that they do not understand. They do not understand what it is like to *see* objects.

A blind person may know what it is like to visually experience movement. If he knows what movement is, that is enough. An experience of movement—whether it be visual, tactile, or kinaesthetic—has its qualitative character defined by what it is an experience (representation) of, and if these experiences are all of the same property, they are, subjectively, with respect to this single property, the same kind of experience.[25] In knowing what it is like to visually experience movement, though, a blind person does not necessarily know what it is like to visually experience an object that is moving. For there is more—much more—involved in seeing an object move than experiencing the object's movement. One also experiences the object's shape, size, color, direction of movement, and a host of other properties. This is why seeing and feeling movement are much different even though the same thing (movement) is represented in both modalities. Even when the senses overlap in their representational efforts—as they do in the case of spatial properties—they (McGinn 1991, p. 35) represent different ranges of determinable properties.

In describing a hypothetical film (visual representation) of a bat's sonar perceptions, Akins (1993, p. 264) makes a similar point—that in seeing what the bat senses (via his sonar apparatus) as he swoops about the cave we do not feel the additional "sympathetic sensations" appropriate to such movements. So, in knowing only how his sonar represents his surroundings (the film might give us that), we do not necessarily know what it is like to be a bat. That would require knowing how else the bat was representing his surroundings and his own internal state. I do not know what it is like to be you watching an angry lion charge just because I know what angry lions look like. I also have to know what it is like to sense an adrenalin rush.

4   Consciousness

Some people have cancer and they are conscious of having it. Others have it, but are not conscious of having it. Are there, then, two forms of cancer: conscious and unconscious cancer?

Some people are conscious of having experiences. Others have them, but are not conscious of having them. Are there, then, two sorts of experience: conscious and unconscious experiences?

Experiences are, in this respect, like cancers. Some of them we are conscious of having, others we are not. But the difference is not a difference *in* the experience. It is a difference in the experiencer—a difference in what the person knows about the experience he or she is having.

This point is simple enough. It may even appear obvious. It is, after all, a straightforward distinction between what we are aware of and our awareness of it. Yet, despite G. E. Moore's (1903) meticulous account of this difference, and the disastrous consequences of ignoring it,[1] failure to distinguish the object of awareness from the act of awareness contaminates contemporary accounts of consciousness. This chapter is an attempt to clarify some of these issues and to give, thereby, a fuller picture of the role experience plays in our mental lives.

1   Conscious Beings and Conscious States

Stones are not conscious, but we are.[2] And so are many animals. We are not only conscious (full stop), we are conscious *of* things—of objects (the bug in my soup), events (the commotion in the hall), properties (the color of his tie), and facts (that he is following me). Following Rosenthal (1990), I call all these *creature* consciousness. The word is applied to beings who can lose and regain consciousness and be conscious of things and that things are so.

Creature consciousness is to be distinguished from what Rosenthal calls *state* consciousness—the sense in which certain mental states, processes, events, and attitudes (in or of conscious beings) are said to be either conscious or unconscious. When we describe desires, fears, and experiences as being conscious or unconscious we attribute or deny consciousness, not to a being, but to some state, condition, or process in that being. States (processes, etc.), unlike the creatures in which they occur, are not conscious of anything or that anything is so although their occurrence in a creature may make that creature conscious of something or that something is so.

For purposes of this discussion I will regard "conscious" and "aware" as synonyms when used as transitive verbs. Being conscious of a thing (or fact) is being aware of it. Accordingly, "conscious awareness" and "consciously aware" are redundancies.[3] A. White (1964) describes interesting differences between the ordinary use of "aware" and "conscious." He also describes the different liaisons they have to noticing, attending, and realizing. Though my use of these expressions as synonymous for present purposes blurs some of these ordinary distinctions, nothing essential is lost, I think, by ignoring these nuances.

I assume, furthermore, that seeing, hearing, smelling, tasting, and feeling are specific forms—perceptual forms—of consciousness. Consciousness is the genus; seeing, hearing, and smelling are species. Thus, seeing a person is one way of being conscious of the person. One can also become conscious of the person by feeling, hearing, or smelling him.[4] You may not pay particular attention to what you see, smell, or hear, but if you see, smell or hear it, you are, in the relevant sense, conscious of it.

The words "in the relevant sense" are important. For one can be aware of an F (see or smell an F) without being aware that it is an F—without, therefore, being aware that one is aware of an F (see the earlier discussion of this point in chapter 1, §3). One can be aware of (hear) the sound of a French horn without being aware that that is what it is. One might think it is a trombone or (deeply absorbed in one's work) not be paying much attention at all. If later asked whether you heard a French horn, you might well reply "No." Wrong! Not being aware that you were aware of a French horn does not mean you were not aware of a French horn. Even if you are asked this question, not later, but when you are hearing the French horn, you might (thinking it is a trombone) reply "No." Wrong again! Hearing a French horn is being conscious *of* a French horn—not necessarily that it is a French horn. Mice who hear—and thus become aware of—French horns never become aware that they are aware of anything—much less French horns.

So much for terminological preliminaries. I have, I hope, merely been describing common usage. Given this usage, it may seem natural to suppose that if one is conscious of some object, then one's experience of it must itself be conscious. It may seem natural, that is, to suppose that creature consciousness of something (whether object, event, property, or fact) requires some state in the creature to be conscious. If one hears a piano being played—thus being aware of the piano playing—one's auditory experience of the piano playing must be a conscious experience. If, in the case of dreams and hallucinations, no physical object is actually perceived, a person is still conscious of whatever properties—colors, sounds, shapes, movements—that characterize the experience. The experience of these properties is conscious. For the same reason, if a woman is aware (or simply fears) that someone is following her, then her belief (fear) that someone is following her is a conscious belief (fear).

Though it is"natural" to make this inference, there are dangers in making it. The dangers arise from a possible misconception of what it is for a state to be conscious. For if one thinks of a conscious experience—as many people do—as an experience one is, in some sense, conscious *of*, one necessarily accepts the conclusion that one cannot see a tree or hear a piano without being aware not only of the tree and the piano, but also of one's experience of the tree and piano. This conclusion is most peculiar. It is not to be accepted lightly. It is, in fact, not to be accepted *at all*. There are, to be sure, states in (or of) us without which we would not be conscious of trees and pianos. We call these states experiences. Since these experiences make us conscious of things (pianos, trees, French horns) the states themselves can be described as conscious. But we must be careful not to conclude from this that because the states are conscious, we must, perforce, be conscious of them. That doesn't follow. We are often aware that we occupy such states—that we are experiencing this and thinking that—but that no more makes the states (of which we are aware) conscious than it makes a cancer (of which we become aware) conscious. Conscious mental states—experiences, in particular—are states that we are conscious *with*, not states we are conscious *of*. They are states that make us conscious, not states that we make conscious by being conscious of them. They are states that enable us to see, hear, and feel, not states that we see, hear, or feel.

A point of clarification before we move on to defend this general picture of consciousness. I am not saying that all experiences make one conscious of some *object*. The experiences one has during dreams and hallucinations do not make one aware of any object[5]; yet, these experiences are—or can be—as conscious as veridical experiences. As Millar (1991, p. 2) puts it, "Nothing seems less problematic than that when we perceive something we are in a conscious state which we could be in even if we were not perceiving that thing."

When we are not perceiving anything—any *object*—the experience can be the same as when we are. So if the experience is conscious when we are, then it is also conscious when we are not.

I am not, as I say, denying this. When I speak of experiences making a creature aware of something, I mean to be speaking of the properties, not the objects (if any) the experience makes the creature aware of. In dreams and hallucinations, one occupies representational states that are not "tethered" (by contextual relation C) to an external object—the kind of object these states have the function of informing about. In such cases, the internal representation "says" or "means" that something is pink and rat-shaped, but nothing (to which one stands in the relation C) is pink and rat-shaped. The sensory representation represents$_s$ *this* as having these properties when nothing does (see chapter 1, §4 for this kind of misrepresentation). The person in whom this representation occurs is, to be sure, aware of these properties. They are exactly the properties (pinkness, rat-shapes, etc.) as those who see pink rats are aware of. In the case of hallucination, though there is no consciousness of any object that has these properties.[6] We can, if we like, say that the hallucinator or dreamer is aware of certain images as long as we understand that these "images" are not objects (let alone mental objects) that have the properties one halluci- nates or dreams that something has. They are, instead, the cluster of properties one hallucinates or dreams that some object has. What makes a creature conscious of these proper- ties is the same thing that makes a person who sees pink rats conscious of them: an internal state that represents something to be pink and rat-shaped. Without this represen- tational state, neither the dreamer or the perceiver would experience the properties they experience. Neither would "see" pink rats. The difference between them lies, not in what properties they experience, not in the properties they are aware of, not (therefore) in the qualitative character of their experience, but in what objects they experience. One person sees an object, a pink rat, that has the properties the experience represents something to have. The other does not.

Though I have not explicitly addressed the topic in these lectures, I would say the same about pains, tickles, itches, hunger, thirst, fear, and a variety of other feelings and emo- tions that are commonly thought of as conscious.[7] Pain is not a mental event that is made conscious by one's con- sciousness of it. Just as a visual experience of a tree is an awareness of a nonconscious object (the tree) pain is an awareness of a nonconscious bodily condition (an injured, strained, or diseased part). The qualities we are aware of when we experience pain (thirst, hunger, nausea, etc.) are not qualities of a mental event; they are properties of the physical state of the body an awareness of which *is* the thirst, hunger, or nausea. When things are working right, pains, tickles, and itches stand to physical states of the body (they are experiences of these physical states) the way olfactory, visual, and auditory experiences stand to physical states of the environment. In all cases, the experiences are conscious, yes, but not because we are conscious of them, but because they make us conscious of the relevant states of our bodies. What we are conscious of when we feel pain (hunger, thirst, etc.) are not the internal representations of bodily states (the pains), but the bodily states that these representations (pains) represent. Though we can be—and most often are—aware that we are in pain, pains, like visual experiences, are awarenesses of objects, not objects of which we are aware.

But this, as I say, is a topic I have neither the time nor (I admit) the resources to effectively pursue. Nor do I have anything (plausible) to say about such emotions as joy, despair, dread, and anxiety, which do not—at least not on the surface—have a representational component. So I leave it to others. My project in these lectures is more restricted in scope. It is an argument about sense experience, the kind of internal representation that (normally) makes us aware of external objects. If the argument can be made good with respect to these experiences, then it will be time enough to turn to our experience of internal affairs and, perhaps, even the sort of diffuse emotions and feelings ("diffuse" because not necessarily directed at or upon anything) mentioned above.

As we saw in chapter 1, the type of experience one has is determined, not by the object experienced (there need be no object), but by the properties one's experience represents something to have. If the properties represented are the same, both the person who perceives a pink rat and the person who does not are in the same representational state—hence, the same perceptual state. Both states are conscious (I have alleged) not because the creature in whom they occur is conscious of them (this may or may not be so), but because they make this creature conscious of something. They make one conscious of whatever properties the representation is a representation of and, if there is such, whatever objects (bearing C to the representation) these properties are properties of. That, if you will, is the representational theory of consciousness. Conscious states are natural representations—representations$_s$ in the case of experiences, representations$_a$ in the case of thought. Conscious creatures are creatures in whom such states occur. Call this a *horizontal* theory to distinguish it from the *vertical* theories (HO theories) with which I now contrast it.

2   Higher-order Theories of State Consciousness

David Armstrong (1980, p. 59) has an example that he uses to illustrate the difference between conscious and unconscious experiences. One is asked to imagine a long-distance truck driver:

After driving for long periods of time, particularly at night, it is possible to "come to" and realize that for some time past one has been driving without being aware of what one has been doing. The coming-to is an alarming experience. It is natural to describe what went on before one came to by saying that during that time one lacked consciousness. Yet it seems clear that, in the two senses of the word that we have so far isolated, consciousness was present. There was mental activity, and as part of that mental activity, there was perception. That is to say, there was minimal consciousness and perceptual consciousness. If there is an inclination to doubt this, then consider the extraordinary sophistication of the activities successfully undertaken during the period of "unconsciousness." (p. 59)

In speaking of "minimal" consciousness Armstrong means that the driver was not in a coma or asleep. By "perceptual" consciousness he means that the driver was conscious of other cars, stop signs, curves in the road, and so on. These objects were represented at both the sensory and (in some appropriate way) at the conceptual level. The driver not only saw the other cars, the stop signs, and the curves in the road, he saw them as cars (at least things to be avoided), as stop signs (why else did he stop?), as curves in the road (how else explain why he turned?). Nonetheless, despite possessing these two forms of consciousness, Armstrong thinks there is a form of consciousness the driver lacks. What the driver lacks is introspective awareness, a perceptionlike awareness, of the current states and activities of his own mind. The driver is not aware of his own perceptual activities—that he is seeing the road, the stop signs, the curves. So the driver lacks an awareness of certain items (his own visual experiences) that drivers in more alert states presumably have. If, Armstrong concludes, one is not introspectively aware of a mental state (like the visual experience the driver is having of the road), then it (the experience) is "in one good sense of the word" unconscious. A higher-order awareness of an experience (something the truck driver lacks) is what makes the experience conscious. What the exhausted driver lacks is not experiences of the road, but *conscious* experiences of the road.

Armstrong is here propounding what has come to be called a Higher-Order (hereafter, HO) theory of state consciousness.[8] A mental state (process, attitude, activity) is conscious only if[9] the person (or animal) in whom it occurs is (creature) conscious of it. There are two species of HO theory corresponding to the two senses of "aware" we have already distinguished. HOT (for higher-order thought) theories and HOE (higher-order experience) theories. The first maintains that what makes an experience (the sort of mental state we are here concerned with) conscious is that the creature whose experience it is believes, knows, or somehow conceptually represents this experience (or itself as having this experience). There must be a higher-level thought (or thoughtlike state) that takes, as its object (what it is a thought about) the (lower-level) experience. According to HOT, the truckdriver's experience of the road is nonconscious if the driver is not aware of having (i.e., aware that he has) such an experience. What makes the sensory representation (of the road) conscious is this higher-level conceptual representation of it. David Rosenthal (1986, 1990, 1991, 1993b) has been an articulate spokesman for such a view.

Armstrong (1968, 1980) himself is perhaps[10] better thought of as a HOE theorist. Lycan (1987, 1992) is another such theorist and he describes the theory as a "Lockean inner sense" theory of state-consciousness. The idea behind this variant is that a mental state becomes conscious by one's having a higher-order perception (hence, experience) of it. One monitors the internal environment—one's own experiences and thoughts—with a mental "sense organ" the way one scans the external environment with one's eyes, ears, and nose. What makes the driver's experience of the road conscious is that there is some higher-order sensory, not necessarily conceptual, representation of it. It isn't a higher-order awareness *that* one is experiencing the road that makes the road-experience conscious, but a higher-order awareness *of* the lower order experience. Just as one can smell (be aware of) burning toast, have a sensory representation (i.e., an experience) of burning toast, without knowing what it is, one can, according to HOE theory, be aware of a road experience without knowing or judging that it is an experience (let alone a road experience)—without conceptually representing the road experience as a road experience.

This, as far as I can see, is the only thing that distinguishes HOE theories from HOT theories. HOT theories require, while HOE theories do not, something in the nature of a thought or judgment about a mental state (like an experience) to make that state conscious. HOE theorists do not. This is why some HOT theorists (see, e.g., Carruthers 1989) think animals do not have conscious experiences. Though they may have experiences (e.g., pains), the experiences cannot be conscious because the animals, having no concept of experience (or pain), do not have the requisite higher-order thoughts that they have such experiences. HOE theories, on the other hand, since they require something more in the nature of a sensory (i.e., nonconceptual) relationship to the experience, do not deny conscious experiences to organisms simply on the basis of their lack of appropriate conceptual capacity. You do not have to think, judge, or believe that you are having a certain experience for you to be aware of it (and, hence, for the experience to be conscious) anymore than one has to think, judge, or believe that the toast is burning to be aware of (i.e., smell) it. There is, then, nothing in HOE theories that would preclude animals (not to mention young children) from having conscious experiences and thoughts.

Since HO theories trace the consciousness of a state to some higher-order representation of that state, it is, for purposes of assessing such theories, important to understand *how* the higher-order representations are supposed to represent the lower-order state.[11] If the truck driver's experience of the road is conscious only if the driver is somehow aware of it, how must this experience be represented in the driver's awareness? Must the experience be represented as an experience? As a representation? Would it suffice to represent it as a state of the brain? HO theorists are typically materialists. They identify particular experiences with token states of the brain or nervous system. The truck-driver's experience of the road is, therefore, a material state of his brain. To make this state of the brain conscious, would it be enough for the driver to see (with the help of neurosurgery and mirrors), the relevant state of his brain—thus becoming (noninferentially) conscious of his own experience? If the truck driver became absent-mindedly conscious of his road-experience in this way, in the same way he was conscious of the road, would this make the road experience conscious?

All one can become aware of by scanning (monitoring—choose your favorite word) internal affairs are activities of the nervous system. That, after all, is all that is in there. All that is in the head are the representational vehicles, not the contents, the facts that make these vehicles into thoughts and experiences. You cannot represent a thought or experience *as* a thought or experience, you cannot achieve metarepresentation, by seeing, hearing, smelling or tasting the thought or experience itself. All that experience (in whatever modality) of an experience gives one is a sensory representation of some part of, or process in, the brain. It will not yield a representation of an experience—that part or process in the brain—*as* an experience.

HOE theories appear to be making the mistake of inferring that because mental representations (representational vehicles) are in the head, the mind is there and that, therefore, we can become aware *that* we think and experience (and of *what* we think and experience) by looking within, by experiencing what is inside. That is the same mistake as inferring that because words (meaningful symbols) are in books, the meanings are also there. An internal scanner is as useful in mental affairs as would be a high-resolution camera in deciphering the meaning of coded text. Experiencing (i.e., seeing, touching, etc.) meaningful symbols is not the way to represent their meaning (or the fact that they have meaning). Why, then, should experiencing meaningful brain states—becoming aware of thoughts and experiences—be a way of representing them as mental or as meaningful? But if it isn't, why suppose, as HOE theories do, that higher order experiences of lower-order experiences *make* lower-order experiences conscious? Why should the truck driver's awareness of a process in his brain make that process a conscious thought. My awareness of it[12] would not have this effect. Why should his?

HOT versions of state consciousness avoid the mistake of HOE theories by not insisting on some quasi-perceptual, some sensory, relation to the mental states that are to be made conscious by higher-order awareness. HOT theories require, not sensory awareness of an experience, but a conceptual awareness of it, some thought or judgment that it is an experience (perhaps, an experience of such-and-such kind). Since one can conceptually represent an experience as an experience without an awareness of the experience (see the discussion of displaced perception in chapter 2), one need not, according to a HOT theory of conscious states, be aware of one's own experiences (i.e., sense them) for these experiences to be conscious. All that is necessary is that one be aware that one is having them, and one can be aware that one is in a certain state without being aware *of*, without sensing, the state itself. This, presumably, is how most people find out that they have cancer—not by perceiving the cancer, but by perceiving something else (X-rays? a medical report?) that tells them they have cancer. This possibility makes HOT theories plausible in a way that HOE theories are not.

There are, however, two objections to HOT theories that are, in my mind, decisive. First, as developmental studies show, children only begin to gain a conception of thought and experience (as ways of representing the world that may or may not be accurate) around their third year (Perner 1991; Flavell 1988; Wellman 1990). On a representational theory of the mind, the fact that they only begin to understand the mind at about the same time they begin to understand the concept of representation (see Perner 1991, pp. 82, 189) is, of course, no accident. Given these developmental facts, children before the age of three years are unable to conceptually represent themselves as experiencing or believing things. It is hard to see, therefore, how, at this early age, they could have a higher-order thought of the requisite kind. How could they have higher-order thoughts that things appear to be F—where this is understood to mean that things need not actually *be* F for them to appear that way— if they lack concepts for experience or thought? If they are unable to hold higher-order beliefs about lower order thoughts and experiences, are we to conclude, therefore, that none of their thoughts and experience are conscious? They may not, to be sure, be conscious that they have experiences, but that isn't the question. The question is not whether a two-year-old knows what a six-year-old knows (about its own experiences), but whether the experiences of a two-year-old and a six-year-old are, as a result of this fact, fundamentally different—the one being conscious, the other not. If that is a consequence of a HOT theory, it strikes me as very close to a *reductio* (it would *be* a *reductio* if we really knew—instead of merely having strong intuitions—that their experience was not fundamentally different). If two-year-olds are as perceptually conscious of external events and objects as their older playmates, if they see, hear, and smell the same things (as HOT theory acknowledges to be the case) why should the child's ignorance of the fact that it sees, smells, and hears things render its experience of them unconscious? What is the point of insisting that because they know less about their thoughts and experiences, their thoughts and experiences are different? Why not just say what I just said: that two-year-olds know less about their experience of the world but, barring other deficits (poor eye-sight, deafness, injury, etc.), their experiences are pretty much the same as ours? That is what we say about their diseases. Why not about their experiences? Why collapse the distinction between S's awareness of X and the X of which S is aware in this place, but nowhere else?

The same should be said about animals. I see no reasons to think that because animals have no concept of experience—do not, therefore, know or believe that they have experience—that, therefore, their experience is somehow different from ours. It may be (and probably is) different, of course, but the fact that they have no concept of experience is surely not the reason it is different. When a dog scratches, are we to believe that the itch is not conscious, or that the dog's experience is totally different from ours, because the dog has no conceptual resources for thinking that it is an itch, that it is irritating, or whatever (on a HOT theory) one has to think about an experience to make it conscious?

Rosenthal is aware of these difficulties, of course, and he suggests that, contrary to what I have been arguing, the requisite higher-order thoughts need not be conceptually very sophisticated. In Rosenthal (1991a), for instance, he says that

the higher-order thoughts need only "refer" to lower-order
experience in order to make those experiences conscious,
and a thought can "refer" to an experience without the person (who has the thought) understanding what an experience is. The way this nonconceptualized reference occurs, he
suggests, is the way we can pick out or refer to an object in
our visual field even if we don't know what it is. ". . .
thoughts can similarly refer to sensory states by way of their
position in the relevant sensory field." (32–33) He goes on:
"Something of this sort presumably explains how higher-
order thoughts can be about sensory states even though
conscious differentiation of sensory detail quickly outstrips
our conceptual resources" (33).

This won't do. It is a thinly disguised conflation of higher-order thought with higher-order experience. I can see an
object (off to my left—next to the tree) without knowing
what it is, but if this is the model we are to use to understand the way thought can be about experience without representing the experience *as* an experience, then our relation
to our own experiences is being likened to our relation to
the objects we see and hear. Experiences (and all other
lower-order mental states that become conscious) must be
viewed as existing in a "relevant sensory field" of their own.
This, though, is an "inner sense" theory of what makes a
state conscious. One is asked to imagine an inner eye scanning experiences and becoming "aware" of them without
needing to know what they are in the way I can visually
scan a room full of people without knowing who any of
them are (or even that they are people).

A second objection to HOT theories relates to the fact
that, as Rosenthal admits (see above) "conscious differentiation of sensory detail quickly outstrips our conceptual
resources." Or, as I like to put it there are conscious differ-

ences between experiences of which the experiencer is not conscious: differences in state consciousness for which there is no corresponding difference in creature consciousness. If one grants—as I think one must—that a conscious experience of 8 objects (all of them fully in view; all of them seen) is different from one of 7 objects, then one grants that there are differences in conscious experiences that a person may not know about—may not be conscious of. One grants, in other words, that there are differences in state consciousness for which there is no corresponding difference in creature consciousness. The numbers "8" and "7" are more or less arbitrary. I selected them in order to represent the number of things we all think we can see—simultaneously—but about which we can and do make mistakes. We see seven cards, trees, or people and think there are eight. The next time we see eight and think there are eight. No difference in what we think, but a difference in what we see, a difference, therefore, in our conscious experience of the cards, trees, or people. This being so, conscious differences in experience cannot be traced to differences in higher order thoughts about these experiences. This type of argument is more fully developed in Dretske (1993c, 1994).

Dan Dennett (1991) denies that the multiplicity, the richness, the (if you will) eight-ness, is in my experience of the world if it is not in my thoughts about the world. My conscious experiences cannot differ unless my judgments differ.

When we marvel, in those moments of heightened self-consciousness, at the glorious richness of our conscious experience, the richness we marvel at is actually the richness of the world outside, in all its ravishing detail. It does not "enter" our conscious minds, but is simply available. (408)

For anyone willing to admit that *one* object can "enter" a conscious mind, this seems false. The ravishing detail of the world does not cease to exist when I close my eyes. My experience of this ravishing detail does cease to exist when I close my eyes. So the ravishing detail is not only "in" the world. It is "in" my experience of the world. I actually experience this ravishing detail—or a great deal of it. The details I experience, though, are not always reflected in my judgments about the world (or my judgments, if I make them, about my experience). So my judgments do not always—perhaps they never—track my conscious experiences of the world. How, then, can the consciousness of experiences be identified with higher-order thoughts about them?

There are, to be sure, situations in which it seems appropriate to speak of experiences becoming conscious in a way that seems to lend support to HOT intuitions. One may be so absorbed in one's work that one doesn't "hear" the chiming of the clock or the sound of children in a nearby playground. Suddenly, as we like to say, one becomes aware of it—perhaps even becomes aware that one was hearing it (all along) without really being aware of hearing it. One is sometimes even able to count the total number of chimes even though some of them have already occurred (and are no longer audible) after one starts counting. There is a temptation to describe this (along with Armstrong's truck-driver example) as a case of an experience that was, up to the moment one became attentive, unconscious. It then became conscious. What better explanation for why it becomes conscious than that one became conscious of having it.

Or I talk to an old friend whom I haven't seen for many years. He has grown a moustache (got new glasses, etc.) but I do not notice the addition. Later, in thinking about our conversation, I remember seeing the moustache. That is, I remember seeing something that, at the time, I was unaware of seeing. I realize I was having a certain kind of experience, a moustache-experience if you will, that, at the time I was having it, I was unaware of having. Are not these experiences unconscious at the time I have them? If so, isn't this fact to be explained by the fact that I was not aware of having these experiences at the time I was having them?

Such phenomena are certainly common enough, and I do not wish to deny their occurrence. We do become conscious of having experiences that, at the time they are occurring, we are not conscious of having. We even have experiences that we never become conscious of having.[13] Certainly animals and small children do. But this is no reason to suppose that the experiences themselves are different from the experiences we know about. I sometimes become conscious of coins in my pocket (stains on my tie, etc.) that I did not realize were there. The coins (stains) are still the same. It is *me* that is different. I know something I did not know before. We must not project differences in us—the knower—onto the objects we know about. This is especially true of mental affairs where the possibilities for confusion are so much greater. If we do not carefully distinguish consciousness of X from the X of which we are conscious, then creature unconsciousness—the fact that one is not conscious of X—can easily be mistaken for state unconsciousness—that the X itself is unconscious. Hearing a clock chime—thus having an auditory experience of these events—does not require you to know or be aware that you are hearing a clock chime— that you are having auditory experiences of such-and-such kind. Mice can hear the clock chime and they are not aware that they are hearing a clock chime or, indeed, that they are hearing anything at all (I assume here that mice do not have the concept of *hearing*). They are as conscious of the chimes as we are. What happens after we "wake up" and realize that we have been seeing or hearing something for a long time (mice never do "wake up" and realize this) is a change in creature consciousness, not state consciousness. No state of us changes from unconscious to conscious. The person becomes conscious of certain experiences (in the sense of becoming conscious *that* she is having them) that she was not conscious of before. These changes in creature consciousness—changes in what one is aware of—involve changes of state (acquiring a belief that one did not have before), but not necessarily any change in the state of which one becomes conscious.

The experience of eight objects and the experience of seven objects are different conscious experiences, not because one is aware that they differ, but because these experiences make one aware of different things—eight objects in the one case, seven in the other. Hearing the clock chime without realizing that it is chiming (or that one is hearing it) involves conscious auditory experiences because these experiences makes one (the person in whom they occur) aware of the chimes. Aware of the chimes—not, mind you, that they are chimes or that one is hearing them. One needs no higher order thoughts to have conscious experience of things. All one needs is experience of things. Conscious states are the ones that make you conscious of things.

3   The Function of Consciousness

One of the benefits of thinking about consciousness in the way proposed here is that it yields a plausible and natural answer to questions about the function or purpose of consciousness.[14] If some mental states and processes are conscious, others not, one can ask, along with Rugg (1992, p.

275), whether conscious ones are more effective than unconscious ones. What is the point, the biological advantage, of having conscious states and processes? Those that are conscious must differ in some relevant way from those that are not. If this is not the case, then, as Davies and Humphrey (1993b, pp. 4–5) conclude, too bad for consciousness: "Psychological theory need not be concerned with this topic."

HO theories of state-consciousness make questions about the function of consciousness hard to answer. Or, worse, they make the answer obvious: it has no function. If what makes E (some experience) conscious is the fact that S (the person in whom the experience occurs) is, somehow, aware of E, then it is clear that E's causal powers (as opposed to S's causal powers) are unaffected by the fact that it is conscious. The causal powers of a rock (as opposed to *my* causal powers) are not changed or enhanced by my observing the rock or having thoughts about it. Why should the causal powers of a thought or an experience be any different? If the consciousness of mental states and processes comes down to higher-order experiences of them, or higher-order thoughts about them, then consciousness is epiphenomenal.[15] Mental states and processes would be no less effective in doing their job—whatever, exactly, we take that job to be—if they were unconscious. According to HO theories of consciousness, asking about the function of conscious states in mental affairs would be like asking what the function of conscious diseases—those we knew about—was in medicine.

But if a mental state is rendered conscious, not by its possessor being conscious of it, but by its making its possessor conscious of something *else*—whatever it was the state represented—then the value of a conscious state or process would reside in what it makes its possessor conscious of.

And here the answer to questions about the biological function of consciousness would appear to be obvious. If animals could not see, hear, smell, and taste the objects in their
environment (all species of consciousness), how could they
find food and mates, avoid predators, build nests, spin
webs, get around obstacles, and, in general, do the thousand
things that have to be done in order to survive and multiply.
Let an animal who is aware of its enemies—where they are
and what they are doing—compete with one who is not and
the outcome is clear. The one who is aware will win hands
down. *That*, surely, is why animals are conscious. Take away
perception—as you do, according to the present theory,
when you take away conscious states—and you are left with
a vegetable.[16]

   This, I expect to hear, is too quick. The question is (or, for
some people, may be) not what the evolutionary advantage
of perception is, but what the evolutionary advantage of
sense perception, of experience, is. After all, in the business
of avoiding predators and finding mates, what is important
(one might suppose) is not seeing a hungry lion (sensuously
representing a hungry lion) but knowing (seeing) that it is a
hungry lion, knowing (seeing) where it is and where it is
headed—i.e., conceptually representing it in some behavior
relevant way (as a hungry lion, dangerous, headed this way,
or whatever). Seeing hungry lions and conceptually representing them as tawny objects or a large shaggy cats (something a two-year-old child might do) isn't much use to one
who is on the lion's dinner menu. It isn't what you see that
is important in the struggle for survival, it is what you know
about what you see. Seeing or smelling poisonous mush-
rooms is no help to one who cannot see or smell (thereby
coming to know) that they are poisonous. It is the representation of one animal by another *as* a receptive mate, not sim-

ply the sense perception of receptive mates, that is important in the game of reproduction. As we all know from long experience, it is no trick at all to see sexually willing (or, as the case may be, unwilling) members of the opposite sex. The trick is to see which is which—to know that the willing are willing and the others are not. That is the skill—and it is a cognitive skill—that gives one a competitive edge in sexual affairs. Good eyesight, a discriminating ear, and a sensitive nose is of no help in the competition if experience always (or often) yields false beliefs about the objects perceived. It is the conclusions, the beliefs, the knowledge, that is important, not the experiences that normally give rise to such knowledge. So why do we have experience? Why are we conscious of objects and their properties—the lion; its color, size, location, and movements—as well as certain behavior-relevant facts about these objects—that (for instance) there is a lion in front of us, that it is moving toward us, and so on? Why aren't we all, in each sense modality, the equivalent of blindsighters who (it seems) get information about nearby objects (indicated by statistically significant performance toward those objects) needed to determine appropriate action without experiencing (seeing) them.[17] If a person can receive the information needed to determine appropriate action,[18] without experience, why don't we? If people can discriminate wavelengths, the sort of discriminations normally found only in those who can perceive colors, without color experience (Stoerig and Cowey 1992), why doesn't everyone? What use is experience in cognition if the same job (the processing of information needed for the determination of appropriate action) can be achieved without it?

These are respectable questions. They deserve answers—scientific, not philosophical, answers. But the answers—at least in a preliminary way—would appear to be clear. There is an enormous number of disabilities—not the least of which (Marcel 1988a) is an inability to initiate intentional action with respect to those parts of the world of which they are not conscious. Humphrey (1970, 1972, 1974) worked (for seven years!) with a single monkey, Helen, whose capacity for normal vision was destroyed by surgical removal of her entire visual cortex. Although Helen originally gave up even looking at things, she regained certain visual capacities.

She improved so greatly over the next few years that eventually she could move deftly through a room full of obstacles and pick up tiny currants from the floor. She could even reach out and catch a passing fly. Her 3-D spatial vision and her ability to discriminate between objects that differed in size or brightness became almost perfect. (Humphrey 1992, p. 88)

Nonetheless, after six years she remained unable to identify even those things most familiar to her (e.g., a carrot). She did not recover the ability to recognize shapes or colors. As Humphrey described Helen in 1977 (Humphrey 1992, p. 89),

She never regained what we—you and I—would call the sensations of sight. I am not suggesting that Helen did not eventually discover that she could after all use her eyes to obtain information about the environment. She was a clever monkey and I have little doubt that, as her training progressed, it began to dawn on her that she was indeed picking up "visual" information from somewhere—and that her eyes had something to do with it. But I do want to suggest that, even if she did come to realize that she could use her eyes to obtain visual information, she no longer knew how that information came to her: if there was a currant before her eyes she would find that she knew its position but, lacking visual sensation, she no longer *saw* it as being there. . . . The information she obtained through her eyes was "pure perceptual knowledge" for which she was aware of no substantiating evidence in the form of visual sensation. . . .

If we follow Humphrey and suppose that Helen, though still able to see where objects were (conceptually represent them as there), was unable to see them there, had no (visual) experience of them, we have a suggestion (at least) of what the function of experience is: to help in the identification and recognition of objects. Remove sensation from S and S might still be able to tell where things are, but S will not be able to tell what they are. At least Helen couldn't. That is— or may be—a reasonable empirical conjecture for the purpose of experience—for why animals (including humans) are, in perception, conscious of objects and their properties.

Despite the attention generated by dissociation phenomena, it remains clear that people afflicted with these syndromes are always "deeply disabled" (Weiskrantz 1991, p. 8). Unlike Helen, human patients never recover their vision to anything like the same degree that the monkey did. Though they do much better than they "should" be able to do, they are still not very good (Humphrey 1992, p. 89). Blindsight subjects cannot avoid bumping into lampposts, even if they can guess their presence or absence in a forced-choice situation. Furthermore, "All these subjects lack the ability to think about or to image the objects that they can respond to in another mode, or to inter-relate them in space and in time; and this deficiency can be crippling" (Weiskrantz 1991, p. 8). This being so, there seems to be no real empirical problem about the function, or at least a function, of sense experience. The function of sense experience, the reason animals are conscious of objects and their properties is to enable them to do all those things that those who do not have it cannot do. This is a great deal indeed. If we assume (as it seems clear from these studies we have a right to assume) that there are many things people with experience can do that people without experience cannot do, then *that* is a perfectly good answer to questions about what the function of experience is. That is why we, and a great many other animals, are conscious of things. Maybe something else besides experience would enable us to do the same things, but this would not show that experience didn't have a function. All it would show is that there was more than one way to skin a cat—more than one way to get the job done. It would not show that the mechanism that did the job didn't have the function of doing it.

The moral of this story is that in seeking a biological function for consciousness, what we should be looking for is a biological function for creature consciousness. If there is a biological purpose, some competitive advantage, in having animals aware of what is happening around them, then, since conscious states are simply the states that make one conscious, there is a biological purpose, the same purpose, for state consciousness. The function of conscious states is to make creatures conscious—of whatever they need to be conscious to survive and flourish. There would only be a problem about the function of conscious states and processes if there was a problem about the advantages of seeing, smelling, and hearing.

5   Externalism and Supervenience

The Jean Nicod lectures (chapters 1–4) were designed, as Johnny Mercer's lyrics put it, to ac-cent-u-ate the positive. It is time to e-lim-i-nate the negative.

My strategy in these lectures was to promote a naturalistic theory of the mind and, in particular, a naturalistic account of experience, by showing how it provides satisfying explanations of a variety of otherwise baffling phenomena—intentionality, self-knowledge, subjectivity, the possibility of qualia-inversion, the sensation-cognition distinction, and so on. Theories that are known to be false, however, do not explain anything. There is a rumour going around that a representational theory is known to be false—if not *of* thought, then certainly *of* experience. It cannot be a correct account of the qualitative aspect of our mental life. If this is so, then, of course, it does not explain anything. The first four chapters are an empty exercise. It is time to confront and, if possible, spike this rumor.

Many of the doubts about the adequacy of a representational theory spring from more general doubts about the adequacy of any externalist theory of sensation. I keep reading that the quality of experience—how things seem to the experiencer, what it is like to *be* the experiencer—cannot be reduced to the way internal events are (or were) related to external affairs.[1] Not only are experiences, like thoughts, inside the head, what makes them the experiences they are—unlike what makes thoughts the thoughts they are—is also in there.

I dealt with one such objection in chapter 2. The fact that experiences are identified and individuated by their relational properties (what they have the systemic function of indicating = what they represent$_s$), does not prevent the person in whom they occur from knowing what kind of experience he or she is having. You are in a better position than I to know what is going on in your mind—what sensations you are experiencing—even though what is going on in your mind is not in your head.

That, though, is only one of the objections to externalism and, therefore, to a representational account of the present type. It is the task of this final chapter to show that these problems are manageable. It is not enough to say—as I have sometimes been tempted to say—that all plausible theories of the mind have the same problems and that, therefore, these problems should not be *my* problems. Since I think the only plausible theories of the mind are externalist in nature, this may be true, but it is not much of a defense. Critics will be quick to point out that it is an admission that all plausible theories of the mind are false.

1   Seeming and Supervenience

The Representational Thesis is an externalist theory of the mind. It identifies mental facts with representational facts, and though representations are in the head, the facts that make them representations—and, therefore, the facts that make them mental—are outside the head. A state of the brain is an experience only if it represents the world in a certain way, and a state represents the world in this way, or so I have claimed, only if it has an appropriate information-carrying function. Since functions (whether systemic or acquired) have to do with the history of the states and systems having these functions, mental facts do not supervene on what is in the head. What is in heads A and B could be physically indistinguishable and yet, because these pieces of gray matter have had relevantly different histories, one is a representational system, the other is not; one is the seat of thought and experience, the other is not; one makes the person in whom it occurs aware of the world, the other does not.

For most philosophers these are unpalatable consequences. This is putting it charitably: for many they constitute a *reductio ad absurdum* of externalist theories of sensation. Even if one agrees with Putnam (1975) that "meanings ain't in the head" and finds Tyler Burge's (1979, 1982) examples in support of the social character of thought (a version of externalism) convincing—thus finds oneself accepting the idea that thought (or some thoughts[2]) have a content determined by external factors—few are willing to say the same about sensations. If two individuals are physically the same, then, surely, the fact that they live in different habitats, the fact that they have had different individual histories, or the fact that they evolved in different ways, is irrelevant to their current experiences. If one has a headache, so does the other. If one is having an auditory experience as of a piano being played (whether veridical or not), so is the other. Even if thought depends on the environment in which one exists (or existed), feelings do not. Theories that deny this are not *just* implausible, they are false. It is all very well for a theory to have materialistically attractive consequences. Other things being equal, these would be reasons for materialists to accept the theory. If the theory were true, it would provide explanations of these facts. Ah, but there's the rub. If it were true! The Representational Thesis cannot be true if it makes what one is experiencing here and now depend—not just causally (no one denies this), but as a matter of logic—on what happened yesterday or in the remote past.

Not only does the Representational Thesis make *what* one thinks and feels externally determined, *that* one thinks and feels is likewise hostage to environmental and historical circumstances. Steve Stich's (1983) Replacement Argument dramatizes this fact. Imagine replacing a thinking-feeling being—you, say—with a duplicate, a "person" that not only lacks your history,[3] but lacks *any* history that would give its information-providing systems the relevant biological and learning-theoretic functions. Such a being would get the same information you get (through its "eyes," "ears," and "nose"), but these systems, lacking the appropriate history, would not have the biological function of providing information—at least not if biological functions are understood (as here understood) as products of a certain selectional process (see chapter 1, §2). The "senses" (if we can any longer call them that) of your duplicate would not generate representations. They would, to be sure, supply the information needed to drive the motor programs in ways that mimicked your behavior, but there would be no internal representations of the objects about which information was delivered. There would, therefore, be no experiences *of*, no beliefs *about*, no desires *for*, these objects. There would be no qualia.

Putnam's Twin Earth examples have convinced many that the mental does not supervene—at least not *locally*—on the physical. That is to say, it does not supervene on the physical constitution of the person having the thoughts. Fred and Twin Fred can be physically indistinguishable (in all intrinsic respects) and, yet, one be thinking that the liquid he sees is water, the other not. The content of thought, at least as it is understood in our commonsense folk psychology, is determined, among other things, by the causal relations that exist—and, just as importantly, *existed*—between events currently occurring in the brain and the person's physical surroundings. Since these causal relations can differ (if Fred and Twin Fred grew up—or evolved—in different environments) even when the brains in question are now indistinguishable, thoughts (understood as *what* is thought—i.e., thought *content*) "ain't in the head." Physically indistinguishable heads can harbor different thoughts.

I begin my defense of externalism—and, therefore, a representational theory of experience—by taking this much externalism for granted.[4] I know that not everyone is comfortable with this result. Some flatly reject it. But I have to start someplace, so I start here. I am arguing with those who think that although an externalist theory of thought may be true, an externalist theory of experience cannot be true. I am arguing the contrary: that if an externalist theory of thought can be true, an externalist theory of experience can also be true. I will have nothing to say to those who reject all forms of externalism, who think that physically indistinguishable beings must be in all the same mental states. I'm trying to win a battle, not the war.

The refusal to tolerate externalism about sensation derives, I suspect, from a certain traditional picture of how we come to know what our experiences are like. According to this familiar story, experiences are subjective surrogates (sense-data, percepts, or what have you) that the mind becomes directly aware of in (indirectly) perceiving the external world. The experience we mean to be describing when we describe ourselves as seeming to see a red ball is identified with either an internal image (a sense-datum) or the mind's awareness of this image. If this datum, this internal image, is red and bulgy, the external object that caused it (if there is one) is also probably red and bulgy—maybe a tomato. For an object to *look red* is for it to cause a red datum to appear in the theater of the mind. The mind, the only spectator in this theatre, becomes directly aware of this datum—its color and shape—and only indirectly ("inferentially") of the properties of the external object that caused it. On this way of thinking about experience, an object's looking red is constituted by direct and infallible awareness of an internal object, the sense datum, that is red.

If this is what is involved in something's looking red, then it is hard to see how something could look red to Fred, green to Twin Fred if they are in the same physical state. For if it looks red to Fred, then Fred must be directly aware of something internal that is red. Twin Fred, on the other hand, must be aware of something green. Since they have different things inside them, they cannot—at least not if materialism is true—be in the same physical state. If they are in the same physical state, things must seem the same to both of them.

This argument doesn't work with thoughts because thoughts are not conceived of as having the properties that objects (thought about) are thought to have. Thinking that *k* is red is not itself red. Thinking that *k* is green is not green. It is, in fact, not quite clear how thoughts must differ in their intrinsic properties to be different thoughts. Maybe thoughts are like utterances; two utterances (in different languages, say) could be the same (consist of the same sounds) and, yet, express quite different propositions, make quite different assertions. Maybe thoughts are like that: the same physical "utterances" occur in two heads and, yet, because they are in "different languages," they manage to *be* different thoughts (have different content). But an experience of red and an experience of green, it will be said, are not like that. They *must* differ intrinsically. Why? Because an experience of red and an experience of green, unlike a thought about red and green, are constituted by an awareness of an internal image or datum that *is* the color the experience is of. Since the image or datum we experience when we experience different colors is subjective—and, therefore, internal—different color experiences cannot occur in indistinguishable beings.

If one conceived of sense-experience in this way, *if* one took a phenomenal appearance to be an internal object (or an awareness of an internal object) that *had* the properties things appeared to have, it would be understandable why one would regard an externalist theory of experience as incoherent. But, as we all know, one person's modus ponens is another's modus tollens. This argument is as lame—and that is very lame, indeed—as is a sense-datum theory of perception. Nobody—at least none of the people I am arguing with—is going to object to a representational account of experience because it is incompatible with a sense-data theory of perception.

But this is not an argument. It is only a speculation about a possible motivation, a speculation about why some philosophers might resist an externalist account of experience without resisting an externalist account of thought. The resistance, I submit, may be traceable to an implicit commitment to an act-object view of sense experience, a view of experience that regards different experiences as experiences of different internal objects. If that is, indeed, the (or a) motivation for the resistance, my hope is that exposure—making it explicit—will suffice to eliminate it. If different sense experiences are not experiences of different internal objects, why should we suppose that persons that do not differ internally could not have different experiences? They can have different parents, wives, and friends—not to mention thoughts and desires—without differing internally. Why not different experiences?

But enough about possible motivations. What about arguments? Let me begin with Fred and Twin Fred, physically indistinguishable fellows who, because they have had different histories, currently have different thoughts. Fred thinks that yonder stuff is flim, Twin Fred thinks it (the *same* stuff) is flam.[5] Given my polemical purposes, this is an admissible way to set the stage. With the stage so set, what, if Fred thinks about it, will he think he is thinking? Will it be the same as what Twin Fred, if he thinks about it, will think he (Twin Fred) is thinking? Insofar as they have introspective access to their own thoughts, will what it seems like to Fred that he is thinking be the same or different from what it seems like to Twin Fred that he is thinking? This is not an epistemological question. It is not a question about how (or even whether) they could find out that what they think they think is different. It is a question of whether what Fred thinks he (Fred) is thinking is the same or different from what Twin Fred thinks he (Twin Fred) is thinking.

A moment's thought (not to mention the results from chapter 2, §3) should be enough to convince one that what Fred thinks he (Fred) is thinking will not be the same as what Twin Fred thinks Twin Fred is thinking. Though physically indistinguishable, their mental states will, in this sense, seem (i.e., seem$_d$[6]) different to them. Fred's lower order thought is that k is flim. His higher-order thought must be that what he is thinking about k is that it is flim since the concepts available to Fred to represent what he is thinking about k are exactly the same as those available to him for thinking about k. If (as we assume) Fred does not have the concept FLAM, he certainly cannot be thinking that he is thinking k is flam. Nor can he be wondering whether he is thinking k is flim or thinking it is flam. If one cannot think anything is flam, one cannot think (or doubt) one is thinking something is flam. So Fred will think he is thinking k is flim. For exactly the same reasons, Twin-Fred will think he (Twin Fred) is thinking it is flam. So what they think they are thinking is different.

Imagine two people making the same noises: they both say that k is "flum" ("flum" is the sound they both make when they say what k is). One person means flim by "flum," the other means flam. Ask the first what he said. He will say he said it was "flum" (this is the sound he will make in telling you what he said k was). Ask the second what he said. He will say he said it was "flum" (this is the sound *he* will make when he tells you what he said k was). Is what they said they said different? Yes. Though the sounds they make in telling you what they said are the same, what they say in making these sounds is different. The first reports that he said it was flim, the second that he said it was flam. The same is true of Fred's and Twin Fred's beliefs about their beliefs. Though not apparent from the activities in their brain (these, we are assuming, are the same), what they think they think is different. Fred's higher-order belief "says" he believes the stuff is flim while Twin Fred's higher-order belief "says" he (Twin Fred) thinks it is flam.

So Fred and Twin Fred not only have different beliefs about the same stuff, they say and believe different things about their beliefs. Not only does k look_d different to them (perception of k prompts them in them different beliefs about k) but, in so far as one can speak of how their own mental processes appear$_d$ to them, their own thoughts seem$_d$ different to them. Fred seems$_d$ (to Fred) to be believing that k is flim while Twin Fred seems$_d$ to Twin Fred to be believing that k is flam.

None of this should be surprising. We have merely been examining the way differences in thought content (at the first order) ramify throughout higher levels of thought. If Fred and his twin believe different things about k, then if they have beliefs about their beliefs, they will believe they believe different things. Such differences in their (first order) mental states will "show up" in differences in what they believe and say about their (first order) mental states. In the sorts of cases we are imagining (Twin Earth situations) none of this will be apparent from either the outside (to us) or inside (to them). It will be true nonetheless.

This, though, does not address the main question—the phenomenal quality of their experience, how things seem$_p$ to Fred and Twin Fred. How things seem$_p$ (unlike how things seem$_d$) is independent of what one believes (or is disposed to believe) about the k one experiences. Just because k looks flim to Fred, flam to Twin Fred, in the *doxastic* sense, just because it prompts them to believe something different, does not mean k looks different to them *phenomenally*, and it is with the phenomenal appearances—the quality of their respective experience, not the content of their respective beliefs—that we are now concerned.

Before we ask whether there is, or could be, a difference in the quality of the twins' experience of k, it is important to note that what Fred and Twin Fred *think* about the quality will differ. Fred will think—correctly as it turns out—that his experience of k is exactly like his experience of flim things. So Fred will think—once again correctly—that k looks$_p$ flim to him. Twin Fred, on the other hand, will think that k looks$_p$ flam to him. He will think—correctly—that k looks the way flam things have always looked to him in normal conditions. So the twins will not only have different beliefs about their beliefs, they will also have different beliefs about their experiences. How their phenomenal experiences seem$_d$ to them is different.

It may be supposed that this does not follow. Just because flim things are not flam things does not mean that flim things do not *look* (phenomenally) like flam things. Babs and Betsy are not the same person, but, being twins, they look alike. Although believing someone is Babs is not the same as believing it is Betsy, believing k looks$_p$ like Babs is the same as believing k looks$_p$ like Betsy since Babs and Betsy look$_p$ the same. For the same reason, Fred's belief that k looks$_p$ flim is really no different from Twin Fred's belief that k looks$_p$ flam. If Fred thinks that k looks$_p$ flim and Twin Fred thinks k looks$_p$ flam, then what Fred and Twin Fred think about the look$_p$ of k is the same.

This is not so. The belief that k looks like Babs is a different belief from the belief that k looks like Betsy even if, in fact, Babs looks like Betsy. Even if, in fact, Babs *is* Betsy. And we are now making a claim, not about the look$_p$ of Babs and the look$_p$ of Betsy (these may be the same), but about the looks$_p$-like-Babs-belief and the looks$_p$-like-Betsy-belief. *These* are clearly not the same. I can have the one belief without having the other. So the twins' beliefs about their experiences of k, about the way k looks$_p$ to them, must be different. As a result of his perception of k Fred is prompted to have a looks$_p$-like-flim belief about k while Twin Fred, seeing the same k, is prompted to have a looks$_p$-like-flam belief. Hence, their phenomenal experience of k seems$_d$ different to them.

It prompts them to have different beliefs about their own experience of k. Hence, even if they have the same phenomenal experience of k, it will not seem$_d$ that way to them.

The access one has to the quality of one's experience (unlike the access one has to the qualities of the external objects the experience is an experience of) is only through the concepts one has for having thoughts about experience.

As we have already argued (see chapters 2 and 4) one does not experience one's experiences (of puddles) in the way one experiences puddles. Hence, there is no way one can become aware of the phenomenal character of one's experience of a puddle (as one can become aware of the qualities of the puddle itself) except through a belief that it has this quality—except, that is, by becoming aware *that* something looks$_p$ to have this quality. By experiencing (e.g., seeing) a puddle one can be made aware of its watery qualities (i.e., it can look$_p$ like water) without possessing the concept WATER, without (therefore) the puddle looking$_d$ like water. One cannot, however, become aware of the watery *look$_p$* of the puddle without this concept. For with no experience of one's experience, awareness of the watery look$_p$ of the puddle can only be awareness *that* the puddle looks$_p$ like water—that one is having an experience of this kind. And *this* requires the concept WATER.

What this means is that if k does not look$_d$ F to S, then, even if it looks$_p$ F, S will not be aware of this fact. If we imagine, furthermore, that the reason k does not look$_d$ F is that S completely lacks the concept of F so that nothing *can* look$_d$ F to S, then although something can still look$_p$ F to S, S cannot be made aware of this fact. Without the concept of F, S is "blind" to the F-aspect of his phenomenal experience (though not, of course, to the F-aspect of the external objects this experience is an experience of). He cannot be made conscious of it. His experience can *have* this quality—things can look$_p$ F to him—but he cannot be made aware of it. With apologies to Kant, without concepts we are blind *to* our intuitions.[7]

To illustrate this important result, let us first take a case where k looks$_p$ F to S and though S has the concept F (is, therefore, *able* to believe that k is, or looks$_p$, F), nothing looks$_d$ F to S.[8] You hold up seven fingers, and I see all seven. Without enough time enough to count, but enough time to see all seven, I mistakenly take there to be eight. That is how many I think I saw. When asked how many fingers there appeared to be, I say eight. That is how many I think there were. That, therefore, is how many there appeared$_d$ to me to be. But how many did there appear$_p$ to me to be? What are the *phenomenal* facts? Believing I saw eight fingers, I will (if I understand the question) describe the phenomenal appearances by using the number "eight." I have no choice. If I didn't think there appeared$_p$ to be eight fingers, why would I think that I saw—and that, therefore, there were—eight fingers? I must think the fingers produced in me an experience of the kind that eight fingers normally produces in me. In this case, though, I am wrong. Given that I saw only seven, the correct answer to how many fingers there appeared$_p$ to be is "seven."

At the phenomenal level seeing (exactly) eight fingers is not the same as seeing (exactly) seven fingers. How could it be? There is as much difference between seeing eight fingers and seeing seven fingers as there is between seeing one finger and seeing two fingers. The only difference is that, as the numbers get larger, the difference is harder to appreciate, harder to detect, harder to notice. As the numbers grow larger, things do not as easily seem$_d$ to be what they seem$_p$ to be. Since, then, one experience is different from the other, there is a fact about my phenomenal experience—that there appears$_p$ to me to be seven fingers—of which I am not aware. Knowing how to count—having the concept of SEVEN—I can, of course, *become* conscious of (i.e., learn) this fact by *counting* the fingers.[9] I will then become aware that my conscious experience of the fingers (before I counted) was not what I took it to be: it was a seven-finger experience, not (as I took it to be at the time) an eight-finger experience. Hence, when the way things seem$_p$ ≠ the way things seem$_d$, the experienc*er* is necessarily unaware of how things seem$_p$. If things seem$_p$ F to S, S is not aware that this is so.

Consider, next, a case in which S lacks the relevant concept—the concept needed to make *k* appear$_d$ to S to have the properties it appears$_p$ to S to have. We are listening to a recording of Goible's 93d Symphony. Thinking there has just been a change of key, but uncertain about it, you turn to me ask whether it didn't sound that way to me.[10] I am musically ignorant. I do not know what a change of key is, and I do not know what a change of key sounds like.[11] So I answer "No" to your question. It did not sound *to me* like they changed key. If truth be told, nothing ever sounds like a change of key to me. To suppose that anything sounds like a change of key to me—someone ignorant of what a change of key is and what a change of key sounds like—is like supposing that an attractive young woman looks like your sister to me. If I don't know who your sister is or what she looks like, how can anyone look like your sister to me?

Clearly, in this exchange about the music, I am describing how things sound$_d$ to me—what I believe, or would normally believe, about what I hear on the basis of hearing it. But if we take your question to be a question not about how the music sounds$_d$ to me, but how it sounds$_p$ to me, about my auditory experience, then the answer is not so clear. Not knowing what a change of key sounds like, *I* am not an expert on what the music sounds$_p$ like to me. CHANGE OF KEY is not a concept I have available for describing my auditory experience. Hence, even if the music sounds$_p$ to me exactly the way a change of key sounds to me,[12] I will not, I *cannot*, become aware that this is so. A conceptual deficit "deafens" me, not to the quality (I *hear*—thus I experience—the change of key), but to the fact that I hear it, to the fact that I have an experience of this kind. The fact that a person would not say, does not think, perhaps would even deny, that k looks$_p$ or sounds$_p$ F does not show that k does not look$_p$ or sound$_p$ F. All it shows is that the person is not aware that it looks$_p$ or sounds$_p$ this way. How am I—someone who has never met your sister—supposed to know whether the woman we now see looks$_p$ like your sister to me, whether she is causing in me an experience which is like the experience your sister causes (or would cause) in me under normal viewing conditions? *You* are probably in a better position to tell me whether she looks$_p$ like your sister *to me* than I am. And this holds, not only for concepts like SISTER and CHANGE OF KEY, but for *all* ways of describing the way things look$_p$. If I don't know what it is to be red, I cannot be made aware of the fact that anything looks$_p$ red to me, that my experience has this qualitative character. Without the concepts, things will still look$_p$ red and green to me. I will still be *aware of* these colors. I will be aware of them in the way that I was aware (see above) of seven fingers (when I mistakenly took there to be eight) and a change of key (when I do not understand the quality of sound to which this refers). I will have no awareness *that* I am aware of them. It will seem$_d$ to me as though I am not aware of them.

This is not simply a matter of knowing, or not knowing, the right labels or words for experienced differences. It is, instead, a matter of lacking certain discriminatory powers. We are sometimes aware of a difference between the way two things appear$_p$ (k and h look$_p$ different, and we realize this) without knowing how to describe the appearance$_p$ of either k or h. S can taste the difference between Coke and Pepsi, but he doesn't know which is which. He may not have heard of these soft drinks—may not, therefore, know that *this* is the Pepsi taste and *that* the Coke taste. He can tell the difference, consistently distinguishing Pepsi from Coke, but not know that *this* is the Pepsi and *that* the Coke taste. Nonetheless, if S responds (or can respond; he may not choose to respond) to one taste in a way different from the way he responds to the other, we give S credit for rudimentary knowledge of taste types and, for present purposes, such discriminatory capacities with respect to taste types may be sufficient for crediting S with rudimentary knowledge of what the liquids taste$_p$ like. Coke and Pepsi not only taste$_p$ different to S, they taste$_d$ different—not *as* Coke and Pepsi, of course, but as *this* (call it a P-tasting) liquid and *that* (call it a C-tasting) liquid. Having the words or concepts for Coke and Pepsi (or even for P-taste and C-taste) is irrelevant. The key question is whether S groups or classifies liquids according to taste. If so, then whatever quality or qualities it is that leads him to do so are the qualities that Coke and Pepsi seem$_d$ to S to have. If not, then even if S tastes$_p$ the difference, he won't taste$_d$ it. He will have no thought of the form, "Aha, this is the same as that, and these two are different." *This* is the situation I imagined myself to be in when listening to the music. Even if I heard it, I did not (not even mentally) group or classify changes of key together. I do not, as a result of hearing sounds with this auditory quality, think, believe, or judge them to be the same in some respect. *That*, and not simply because I lacked words for describing a difference I heard, is what made me "deaf" to a change of key. *That* is why it may have sounded$_p$ like a change of key to me without sounding$_d$ like a change of key to me.

Where does this leave us with respect to Fred and Twin Fred? None of this shows—it was not intended to show—that they have different experiences of the puddle, that the puddle looks$_p$ different to them. That was not my purpose. The strategy is not to show that experience is externally grounded, but that it *could* be, and that denials that it could be are based on a faulty picture of the relation between thought and experience. I have tried to do this by showing that qualia—experiential qualities—are not, as it were, on display in the shop window of the mind. Awareness of phenomenal properties (that one is experiencing redness, the taste of strawberries, or a change of key) is not achieved by a process of direct inward inspection, a process in which one becomes aware of the qualities of experience in the way one becomes aware of the qualities of external objects that the experience is an experience of. Awareness of phenomenal properties—that something looks$_p$ red, say—is a much more indirect process, a process that requires the possession and use of the concepts needed to think that something is (or looks$_p$) red. When illumination is normal and there is a red object in front of me, I am made aware of the color red by merely opening my eyes. I do not need the concept RED to see red. But I do need this concept to become aware of the *quale* red, to become aware that I am having an experience of this sort. This being so, qualia (understood as qualities that distinguish experiences from one another) remain "hidden," inaccessible, until one acquires the conceptual resources for becoming aware of them. I can become aware of the *color* red without the concept RED (just as I can be made aware of seven fingers without the concept of SEVEN), but I cannot be made aware of the *quale* red without this concept. For to become aware of the quale red is to become aware *that* one is having an experience of a reddish sort, and this is something one cannot be made aware of without understanding what it means to be red.

If (as we are assuming) Fred and Twin Fred have different concepts for sorting and identifying the objects they perceive, then, even if they are having the same phenomenal experience of k, the quality of this experience that makes it *the same* experience must remain inaccessible to them. They cannot be made aware of it. What Fred's experience seems$_d$ like to Fred will not be what Twin Fred's experience seems$_d$ like to Twin Fred. If, despite this difference in the way their experiences seem$_d$ to them, these experiences are, nonetheless, the same (they are, let us say, both of the Q-ish sort), then the quale Q will be a quality that neither Fred nor Twin Fred can be made aware of. They will be introspectively blind to that aspect of their experience that makes it the same experience. They will be as unaware of the phenomenal quality Q as I was (see above) to a phenomenal change of key. From a subjective standpoint, it will be as if their experience (of the puddle) was not Q.

If a conceptual externalist (that is, an externalist about belief) is willing to accept this result, then she has, I think, capitulated. She no longer has a reason to resist phenomenal externalism (= externalism about experience). For if one accepts the conclusion of this line of reasoning, then the qualities of experience which allegedly must be the same in physically identical persons are qualities that the persons in question, *if* they are conceptually different, cannot be made aware of. If Fred and Twin Fred, though differing conceptually, are having the same experience of the puddle, the respects in which their experiences are the same (call it Q) is not a quality of their experience that they can be made aware of. If it is not something they can be made aware of, why suppose it must be the same?

The conclusion can be put this way. Either phenomenal experiences are identified with thoughtlike entities—such things as potential beliefs (Armstrong 1969), suppressed inclinations to believe (Pitcher 1971) or micro-judgments (Dennett and Kinsbourne 1992)—in which case the conclusion that sensations have their properties externally grounded if thoughts do follows trivially; or (as in the present study) phenomenal appearances (= the way things appear$_p$) are distinguished from thoughts (from the way things appear$_d$). If experiences are distinguished from thoughts, so that k can look$_p$ F to you without your believing, or being disposed to believe, that anything is F (i.e., without anything looking$_d$ F to you), then it turns out that one may be completely unaware of one's qualia (in the way I was completely unaware of the fact that the music sounds$_p$ like it is changing key). If one takes qualitative states as essentially knowable, as many philosophers do, then phenomenal experiences must be externally grounded if beliefs are. If, on the other hand, one is willing to tolerate unknowable qualia, what reason is there to insist that qualia must be *the same* in physically identical beings? Indeed, what better explanation is there for *why* the experience of Fred and Twin Fred seem so different to them than that it is?

2   Replacement Arguments and Absent Qualia

Lightning strikes an automobile junkyard. After the nuts and bolts settle . . . Lo! . . .Twin Tercel—an exact duplicate of my 1981 Toyota Tercel. Lightning can do such wonderful things. Twin Tercel has all the same identifying features: a small rusty scratch on the rear fender, torn upholstery, stone chips in the windshield, a dented bumper. Even the identification numbers, stamped into the engine block, are the same. Only a quick check, back home, is enough to convince me it is, indeed, a duplicate and not my own car miraculously transported to the junkyard by the electrical disturbance.

More careful inspection reveals a minor difference. Tercel's gas gauge works. Twin Tercel's does not. At least some people say it doesn't work. Others are not so sure. Everyone agrees that the pointer on the gauge in Twin Tercel, unlike the one in Tercel, is unresponsive to the amount of gasoline in the tank. What they don't agree about is whether to describe this as "not working." Who (a skeptic asks) is to say that the gauge in Twin Tercel is supposed to register the amount of gasoline? Indeed, who is to say it is a gas gauge? Do "E" and "F" really mean "Empty" and "Full"? Even if they do, why suppose they refer to amount of gasoline? Maybe the gauge is wired wrong: they stand for the amount of brake fluid in the master cylinder or the amount of solvent in the windshield washer reservoir. We know the corresponding part in Tercel is a gas gauge. We know what *it* was designed to do and that *it* wouldn't be "working" if it failed to register amount of gasoline. We know what *its* symbols mean. But nobody designed Twin Tercel. Nobody put the symbols "E" and "F" there. Why, then, suppose they stand for anything? Maybe—who knows?—Twin Tercel also resembles a 1932 Klingon Space Shuttle. What we see as functioning parts of Twin Tercel's exhaust system, the Klingons see as malfunctioning parts of its forward thrusters. As far as the Klingons are concerned, the only thing that is working *right* in Twin Tercel is what we call the "fuel gauge."

Not only were the parts of Twin Tercel not designed to do anything, they are not a copy, an imitation, or a reproduction of anything that was designed to do something. There is, therefore, nothing the parts of Twin Tercel are supposed to be doing, nothing that, by failing to do, would count as their "not working right." We could, of course, give the parts of Twin Tercel a function—the same function the corresponding parts of Tercel have—but, until we do so, nothing can work right in Twin Tercel and, therefore, nothing can work wrong. There is nothing in Twin Tercel that can (as the corresponding parts in my Tercel can) misrepresent anything. If the gauge in my Tercel behaved that way, it would be broken. It would not be working right. It would be misrepresenting the amount of gas in the tank. None of this is true of the part in Twin Tercel. To suppose that Twin Tercel's "gas gauge" is not working right, that Twin Tercel even *has* a gauge, is like supposing that a word has been misspelled when the wind and waves carve out "anser" in the sand of a deserted beach. If I had made those marks, it might have been a misspelling, but, given the origin of the marks, it isn't. It can't be. If gauges and instruments are objects that have a function, something they are supposed to do, there are no gauges and instruments in Twin Tercel—nothing that can, as the instruments in my Tercel can, represent speed, amount of gas, and oil pressure.

If we forget about the gas gauge for the moment (the only point of difference between Tercel and Twin Tercel) Twin Tercel would coast through a Toyota Turing Test. Twin Tercel, after all, is physically, and therefore functionally, indistinguishable from Tercel. You cannot tell them apart. Nonetheless, despite indistinguishability, all is dark in the representational mind of Twin Tercel. Twin Tercel is a Toyota zombie.[13] Tercel has a thermostatically controlled fan that cools the radiator when sensors tell it that the coolant temperature is getting too high. As a result of this arrangement, Tercel, so to speak, fans itself when it thinks it is (i.e., represents itself as) getting hot. It does this whether or not it is getting hot. For the same reason, Tercel also emits a loud screeching sound when it "thinks" the seat belts are not fastened. Tercel comes equipped with "sensors" whose function it is to detect high coolant temperature and unbuckled seat belts and to initiate appropriate responses. Twin Tercel behaves in the same way—fans its radiator when coolant temperature rises and emits a loud screeching sound when seat belts are not fastened—but it doesn't do these things for the "reasons" Tercel does them. There is nothing in Twin Tercel that has the function of registering coolant temperature, nothing that is supposed to detect unbuckled seat belts. There is, as a result, nothing in Twin Tercel that represents the conditions that cause it to behave the way it does. This is why Tercel can be "fooled" and Twin Tercel cannot. Tercel will fan its radiator even when the temperature is normal. It will do so when it "thinks" the temperature is too high. There are circumstances in which Twin Tercel will also fan its radiator when the temperature is normal, but Twin Tercel will not do so because it "thinks" the temperature is too high. There is nothing in Twin Tercel (as there is in Tercel) that means the temperature is too hot when it isn't.

This, it will be said, merely shows that experience is not representational. If Twin Fred materialized in a swamp the way Twin Tercel materialized in that junkyard, Twin Fred would be having exactly the same thoughts and experiences as Fred. If Fred fanned himself because he felt hot, Twin Fred would be fanning himself for the same reason—

because he felt too hot. Physical indistinguishability may not imply representational equivalence if representation is understood the way it is here being understood (i.e., as historically grounded). Tercel and Twin Tercel illustrate that. But it *does* imply an equivalence of experience. So experience is not representational. The quality of experience, what it is like to have an experience, has something—and who knows?—maybe everything to do with the physical constitution of the experiencer. Keep the physical constitution the same and the experiences will also be the same.

This, I assume, will be a widely shared reaction to my story about Twin Tercel. The reaction is so widely shared that it deserves a name. I will call it the Internalist Intuition. The Internalist Intuition gives expression to the conviction that experience (i.e., the quality of experience, what it is like to have the experience) supervenes on the constitution—and for materialists this can only mean physical constitution—of the experiencer. If Fred and Twin Fred are physically the same, they must have the same experiences. If a naturalistic theory of representation makes it the case that Swamp Fred (spontaneously materialized in a swamp the way Twin Tercel materialized in that junkyard) has no sense organs, nothing to provide it with experiences, in the way that Twin Tercel had no gauges to produce representations, this doesn't show (as it did with Twin Tercel) that everything is "dark" in the mind of Swamp Fred. All it shows is that a naturalistic theory of representation is not a satisfactory theory of experience. So says the Internalist Intuition.

The Twin Tercel parable does not directly challenge the Internalist Intuition. It does not show that this judgment is false or even implausible. It was not intended to do this. What it was designed to do, instead, is to reveal how unreliable ordinary intuitions are about miraculous materializations and instantaneous replacements. Our judgments about what it makes *sense* to say—what it would be *true* to say—about such bizarre cases are influenced by factors that, on deeper reflection, we see to be quite irrelevant. We are, for instance, influenced by a striking resemblance in appearance and placement[14] of parts. Yet, no one thinks that because my doorstop looks like your paperweight, and happens to be placed on papers (thus holding them down), that it *is*, therefore, a paperweight. Just because a bushing looks like your wedding ring doesn't mean it *becomes* your wedding ring if you slip it on your finger to keep track of it. Yet, when asked to render judgments about more complex objects—automobiles, for example—we blithely ignore the fact that the resemblance in both appearance and placement is (by hypothesis) completely fortuitous and, thus, irrelevant to determining the function of parts.[15] We ignore this and proceed to assign functions on the basis of resemblance and placement anyway. We seem driven by what I call the Paley Syndrome[16]—an irresistible tendency to use resemblance and placement as a basis for attributing purpose and design. There is, of course, nothing irrational about the Paley Syndrome. It is, in normal circumstances, a perfectly respectable form of analogical reasoning. If I find Twin Tercel in the middle of the desert, I will infer—and I expect that reasonable people will join me in inferring—that it was designed (probably by the same people that designed my 1981 Tercel) and that, as a consequence, *this* (pointing at its lifeless gas gauge) is not working right. This is perfectly reasonable. What is *not* reasonable is to make the same inference when—as in the Twin Tercel story—one is told in advance that the parts were *not* designed, that none of them were made or placed there for any purpose. To persist in giving them a purpose anyway—something one does (if only implicitly) by calling them gauges and instruments—is irrational.

I assume that most readers will have supposed, on first hearing the Twin Tercel story, that it not only made perfectly good sense, but that it was true, to say that Twin Tercel had a broken gas gauge. The Paley Syndrome is such a habitual part of our inferential practice that we use it to generate intuitions about cases even when we "know" it doesn't apply. After thinking about what it takes to be a gauge and about whether Twin Tercel's parts have what it takes, these intuitions, these prereflective judgments, begin to change. At least they become less "intuitive." This is typical of philosophical thought experiments in which one is asked to make judgments about situations that differ profoundly from the familiar regularities of daily life. Intuitions are generated by, they bubble out of, customary patterns of thought, exactly the patterns of thought that are not applicable in the bizarre circumstances characteristic of philosophical thought experiments. The time to *suspend* intuitions, the time to *not* trust snap judgments, is in the midst of a philosophical thought experiment. That is where they are *least* likely to be reliable.

Once again, this is not an argument, merely a plea for methodological caution. There are other reasons to be cautious. We are dealing with cases that combine the most complex problems in epistemology and metaphysics. Even if we had clear and distinct intuitions about Twin Tercel, what do we say if the lightning strikes, not a Toyota-free junkyard, but my Tercel when it is parked in a junkyard? Which of the two resulting Toyotas is my Tercel and which the duplicate? Or is neither a duplicate? Maybe the original split—amoeba fashion—into two Tercels, both of which have the history (and, therefore, gauges and instruments) of the original. We can imagine all kinds of intermediate cases. Even if we have clear and distinct ideas about what it takes to be a gas gauge, do we, in each of these cases, have a clear idea about which of the resulting Toyotas has a gas gauge?

It would be wise, then, to be cautious in our judgments about what must be the case when Swampman (a Donald Davidson doppelganger) materializes in some swamp. We have a right to ask why the Internalist Intuition should be regarded as more reliable than our initial judgments about Twin Tercel. Why must Swampman have all the same thoughts and experiences as Donald Davidson? Indeed, why must Swampman have *any* thoughts and sensations? Is this judgement based on some deep insight about the nature of thought and experience or is it merely a brute intuition, a metaphysical axiom, the sort of fact that is available as a premise, but never as a conclusion, in reasoning about the mind? Brute intuitions are all well and good. We have to start somewhere. Not *all* premises can be conclusions. But such premises are suspect when applied to fantastic situations that violate normal expectations and background presuppositions. It would be silly to wonder whether a stranger found wandering around in my yard, a person that looked and acted exactly like my wife in the kitchen, was completely devoid of feelings and experiences (i.e., a zombie). That is the stuff of Hollywood science fiction, not everyday life. I fail to understand, though, why it would be any more silly than wondering whether an automobile parked in my driveway, one that looks and acts exactly like the one in my garage, really had a carburetor, brakes, and a speedometer. Both possibilities sound silly. Yet, in the second case, the silliness comes, not from the impossibility of a physically indistinguishable car lacking these parts, but from the improbability of the events (spontaneous materialization) that would have this result. What reason is there to think that the silliness of the first isn't the same?

Aside, then, from its intuitive appeal—an appeal that we should mistrust—is there any reason to think the Internalist Intuition valid in the extraordinary circumstances described in Swampman (and similar "replacement") thought experiments?

I have already discussed and, I hope, disposed of two reasons for thinking that the Internalist Intuition is true. There is, first, the argument from self knowledge: the argument that if the quality of one's experience was determined by extrinsic factors (thus making it possible for doubles to have different experiences), it would not be possible to know, by introspection, by looking inward, what it was like to have those experiences? The answer I gave to this objection (in chapter 2) was that although one has privileged information about the character of one's own experiences, one does not look *inward* to get it. Knowledge about one's own experiences is obtained not by experiencing one's experience, but by simply *having* the experience one seeks knowledge of. The experience itself—normally an experience of *external* objects—carries all the information one needs to know what the experience is like. A second possible source for the intuition that experience cannot be extrinsically constituted was discussed in the previous section. If one conceives of experience in act-object terms—as the mind's awareness of *internal* objects or qualities—then it becomes impossible for a materialist to think of Fred and Twin Fred as having different experiences. If different experiences are awarenesses of different internal things, creatures in whom different experiences occur must, on this conception of experience, differ. Fred and Twin Fred *cannot* be having different experiences. The way to shed this prejudice against externalism is quite easy: shed (as almost everyone has) this quaint conception of sense experience.

In the next section I will turn to a third possible source of the intuition that Fred and Twin Fred *must* be having the same thoughts and experiences. This is the idea that if the twins were having different thoughts or experiences, then, since much of what minded creatures do is caused by what they think and experience, one would expect this difference to show up in different behaviors. At least it should be *possible* for it to show up. But, since Fred and Twin Fred are physically indistinguishable, Fred and Twin Fred *cannot* behave differently. So any alleged difference in what they think or experience would have to be completely epiphenomenal: it could never reveal itself in anything they said or did. If nothing the twins can either say or do can evince the alleged mental difference, though, what is the point, what is the sense, in saying that such differences exist? The logical positivists liked to say that a difference that did not make a difference was not a difference at all. That may have been too strong, but, surely, a difference that *cannot* make a difference, not even to the person in whom it occurs, is not a real difference. Or, if it is, it is not one a theory of the mind need worry about.

Aside from these possible grounds for the Internalist Intuition, I can think of no other support for the Internalist Intuition that is not a variation on one of these three themes. I conclude, therefore, that the Internalist Intuition is a *brute* intuition, one that is not justified by any defensible claim about the nature of thought or experience. This does not show that externalism is true and that, as a consequence, physically indistinguishable beings can have different experiences. It does not even show that internalism—especially about experience—is implausible. Not at all. Most philosophers take it as plausible enough not to need argument. Arguments have to stop someplace, and this seems as good

a resting point as any. I confess to myself feeling the pull of
the Internalist Intuition. Indeed, I would not have thought
to question it but for the fact that unless it is challenged, an
even more (for me) obvious fact must be rejected—the idea,
namely, that what goes on in the mind—what we think, feel
and experience—and, therefore, the qualities in terms of
which we distinguish thoughts, feelings, and experiences
from one another, are nowhere to be found in the head—
where the thoughts, feelings, and experiences are. The problems about conscious experience are so baffling that one can
reasonably expect the right answers—if right answers are
ever to be found—will require abandoning *some* deeply held
convictions about the mind–body relation. One will have to
make a hard choice about what to give up. My choice is the
Internalist Intuition.

3 Explanatory Relevance

One reason, not yet discussed, for supposing that externalism is objectionable is that it allegedly makes the mind
epiphenomenal. Causality, it is said (e.g., McGinn 1989; Fodor
1991) is a *local* affair. The causal efficacy of an event resides
in its *intrinsic* properties (and, of course, the circumstances
in which this event occurs). Put the same kind of event—
one with the same intrinsic properties—in the same conditions and it will have the same effects. That is why physical
duplicates—Fred and Twin Fred, for example—behave in
the same way. The internal events that produce their behavior are intrinsically the same. Hence, they produce exactly
the same bodily movements. The internal events and
processes that cause Fred's arm to execute movement M are
exactly the same as those that cause Twin Fred's arm to execute movement M. Since these causal processes are the

same, whatever extrinsic (e.g., historical) differences exist between the events that cause their arms to move must be causally irrelevant to why their arms move the way they do. If the mental is extrinsic, if it does not supervene on the present physical constitution of Fred and Twin Fred, as it clearly doesn't on a representational theory of experience and thought, then it will be irrelevant to why Fred and Twin Fred behave the way they do. The Representational Thesis makes what you think and feel irrelevant—causally irrelevant—to what you do.

Something like this reasoning is probably somewhere in the background when people invoke the Internalist Intuition. Clyde winces because it hurts. He goes to the fridge because he wants a beer. He grabs this bottle, not that one, because he thinks this is the beer and that the catsup. The only way to understand how the pain, the thought, and the desire can explain these behaviors is if the pain, the thought, and the desire are *inside* helping to bring about the associated bodily movements. By locating the mental outside the body, by making what we think, desire, and feel depend on our history, externalism makes such ordinary explanations of behavior sound like magic.

There are several possible confusions in this reasoning, the most important of which is the conflation of behavior with bodily movement. What thoughts, desires, and feelings explain is not why your arm moves (when you move it intentionally), but why you move your arm. Once the difference between behavior and bodily movement is clear, it also becomes clear that externalist theories of the mind are *not* threatened by epiphenomenalism. Mental content can explain behavior without supervening on the neurophysiological events and processes that cause bodily movement. The mental is *not* robbed of its explanatory relevance by being extrinsic.

Before enlarging on this point, though, a clarification. Historical events, things that have happened to a person, things that are, therefore, extrinsic to the current state of the person, can certainly make a causal difference to that person's behavior. Jimmy stutters because he was dropped on his head when he was an infant. We can think of the fall as a remote cause. It produced in Jimmy a permanent neurological condition, N, that now operates as a proximal cause of Jimmy's stutter. We can imagine a twin, someone in the same neurological condition, but who was not dropped on his head. A brick fell on Johnny's head. It produced the same neurological condition that Jimmy suffers from. Same proximal causes, different remote causes. The fact that Jimmy's fall has its effect on Jimmy's behavior through a proximal condition (neurological damage) that can be produced by other causes does not show that the fall is not among the causes of Jimmy's current behavior. It does not show that knowledge of the remote event isn't relevant to understanding why Jimmy stutters. All it shows is that different causes can have the same effect, that different (remote) explanations can explain behaviors that have the same proximal cause.

There is, then, no metaphysical problem in having historically remote conditions acting as causes of current behavior—no problem in conceiving of extrinsic facts—conditions that do not supervene on the *current* state of the system—explaining the current behavior of the system. Remote causes *are* causes even though their effects are brought about via more proximal events. There is, then, no particular problem about conceiving of different explanations for Fred's and Twin Fred's behavior. If Jimmy's fall explains why *he* stutters even though a similar fall does not explain why someone with the same neurological condition stutters, there should be no special problem in accepting the idea that the explanation for Fred's behavior might be much different from the explanation for Twin Fred's behavior even though Fred and Twin Fred (being physically indistinguishable) have the same proximal causes of their behavior.

The objection to the Representational Thesis, then, should not be that it makes extrinsic (i.e., historical) facts relevant to the explanation of a person's behavior. That cannot be the objection since there is nothing objectionable in that. The point is rather that the Representational Thesis somehow makes the *here-and-now* (i.e., proximal) explanatory relevance of experience and thought into a *there-and-then* (i.e., remote) causal relevance. This is objectionable because, as Horgan (1991, pp. 88–89) puts it, one has (at least Horgan has) an "unshakable" conviction that beliefs, desires, and feelings—the *reasons* for which we act—have an "immediate" causal/explanatory relevance to our intended behavior. By making the causal/explanatory relevance of the mind (temporally) remote, the Representational Thesis denies this basic intuition.

Horgan is certainly right about one thing: beliefs, desires, and experiences, the mental states that explain a person's current behavior, must exist at the time of the actions they help explain. Feeling a pain is not going to explain why you wince unless you feel the pain *at the time* you wince. If wanting a glass of beer is to explain a trip to the fridge, then it must exist *in* the head of the trip-taker *at the time* of the trip. If beliefs, desires, and experiences are to explain here-and-now behavior, they have to be here-and-now beliefs, desires, and experiences. This is not in dispute.[17] What *is* in dispute, what (despite Horgan's unshakable conviction) is not so clear, is whether the facts that give mental states their identity, the facts that underlie the content of belief and quality of experience, whether *these* facts have to be here-and-now facts. Do *these* facts have to exist at the time and place of the behavior they explain?

I do not think so, and the reason I do not is that the events that reasons (here-and-now beliefs and desires) cause are not the behavior that reasons (there-and-then content) explains. I have developed this point at great length elsewhere.[18] What I give here is a brief sketch and a few examples. It will be enough, I hope, to indicate the general line of response.

A plant, the Scarlet Gilia, changes color during the summer. This is plant behavior, something the plant does. Plants don't have thoughts and desires, experiences and feelings, but they do things, sometimes very interesting things, and botanists are interested in explaining why plants do the things they do. Why does the Scarlet Gilia do this—change from red to white in the middle of July each year?

One explanation, the one given by Page and Whitham (1985), the botanists from whom I take this example, is that the plant does this in order to attract pollinators. Early in the season hummingbirds are the chief pollinators, and hummingbirds are more attracted to red blossoms. Later in the season the hummingbirds migrate and hawkmoths become the principal pollinators. Hawkmoths prefer white blossoms. The flower changes color "in order to" exploit this seasonal alteration in its circumstances. The plant sets more fruit by changing color, and, in the words of Page and Whitham, this is why it does it.

This explanation of the plant's behavior appeals to there-and-then facts, events in the evolutionary history of the plant that happened long ago and (probably) far away. Explaining the plant's behavior in this way is not, however, to give a remote cause of the plant's change of color. This is not at all like mentioning Jimmy's fall in explaining his stutter. Jimmy's fall produced a neurological condition, N, that causes, in turn, Jimmy's stutter. Giving the adaptive "purpose" for which the plant changes color is not describing a more distant member of a causal chain that has chemical activity in the plant as proximal cause and pigment change as its effect. What the evolutionary process explains is plant *behavior*, why it changes color. This is not what the seasonal changes cause. The seasonal changes cause chemical activity in the plant that produces a pigment change. Natural selection does not cause the chemical changes in the plant that, in turn, bring about a pigment change. What (here-and-now) causes the plant to change color are seasonal changes (longer sunlight, warmer days, the "ringing" of an internal biological alarm clock, or whatever), and natural selection is not the remote cause of these here-and-now seasonal events. What natural selection explains is not, so to speak, what is happening here-and-now, but why one thing that is happening here and now (seasonal changes) causes another here-and-now event (change of color). The causal pattern is not

(A) Natural Selection—>Warm Days—>Chemical
Activity—>Color change
but, rather,

(B) Natural selection—>[Warm Days—>Chemical
Activity——>Color Change]

The brackets in (B) are meant to indicate that what natural selection causes is not the warm days *that* cause color change. It, rather, causes warm days *to cause* color change. Natural selection is, as it were, the cause of one thing (warm days) causing another (color change). What natural selection brings about is a change in the plant's chemical constitution, a condition that explains why the plant behaves the way it does, why it changes color in the summer. That is much different from causing the change of color.

Consider, now, a physically indistinguishable plant, one that is a molecular twin of the Scarlet Gilia. The twin evolved in quite a different environment, an environment in which, in the midst of its flowering season, rapacious beetles arrived that were attracted by red blossoms. As a result of this selectional pressure, a slow change occurred: the plant evolved into a form in which it changed color, from red to white, in the midst of every flowering season. The beetles hate white blossoms. They avoided Twin Plant and it flourished.

Although Twin Plant is physically identical to Scarlet Gilia, and although it therefore behaves in exactly the same way, the explanation of why it behaves this way is quite different. Scarlet Gilia changes color to attract Hawkmoths. Twin Plant changes color in order to repel beetles. You could study these two plants under a microscope for years, know everything there was to know about their present physical constitution, and never realize that there were quite different "reasons" for their behaving the way they do. Although the change in color is a purely physical event, and although it is produced by well-understood chemical changes inside the plant, the explanation of the plant's behavior—why it changes color—does not consist of descriptions of these internal causes. It consists, instead, of descriptions of those events and processes that made these internal events cause that external change. This requires going outside the plant, to something that happened in the history of the plant (or the history of this kind of plant). This "retreat" to there-and-then facts to explain the plant's here-and-now behavior is not—I emphasize *not*—because we (or botanists) hanker after remote causes of current events. For, once again, the adaptive explanation does not provide remote causes of current events. What it provides is an explanation of current behavior, why the current events are causing changes in the plant's color.

Even if you know what physical events inside the plant cause the change in color, you do not necessarily know why the plant changes color. For both the change in Scarlet Gilia and Twin Plant are produced by exactly the same chemical changes. Yet, they did not change color for the same reason. Often, when we are looking for why a system, including a plant, behaves the way it does, we are looking, not for the internal cause of surface change (in the case of the Scarlet Gilia, we already know that). We are, instead, trying to find out why the surface change is being caused. We know that A is causing B. What we want to know is why it is.

We can, if we like, imagine a third plant, Swamp Plant, indistinguishable from the first two, that has *no* reason for changing color. Swamp Plant materialized (conveniently potted) when lightning struck a plant nursery. In the middle of July (just like Scarlet Gilia and Twin Plant) Swamp Plant changes color. Why? Why is Swamp Plant turning white? Is it doing so in order to repel beetles? To attract hawkmoths? No. Swamp Plant, though physically identical to the other two plants, and though, as a result, behaving the same way as these other two plants, does not have the same reasons for behaving this way. It doesn't have any reasons for behaving this way.

Swamp Plant is the botanical analog of an animal doing something mindlessly. When I snore or hiccough, I do something. I do something just as Swamp Plant does something when it changes color in July. But Swamp Plant and I don't have reasons for behaving this way. This is not to say there are not causal explanations for our behavior. It is only to say that, in my case, there is no rational, no purposive, no psychological explanation. In Swamp Plant's case, the behavior has no adaptive purpose, no teleological explanation. Nonetheless, though not purposive, Swamp Plant could pass a botanical Turing Test. It would behave exactly the way an "intelligent" plant—Scarlet Gilia or Twin Plant—behaved. Yet, unlike these other two plants, there would be no purpose in Swamp Plant behaving this way. Swamp Plant is a botanical zombie. Swamp Plant has no reason to change color. If its change of color repels a stray beetle, or attracts some wandering hawkmoths, that is dumb luck, a coincidence. That is not why it does it. The botanical analogue of the Turing Test, just as the original Turing Test, does not test for the right thing. It does not tell us what we want to know: whether the behavior (in the case of plants) is for some purpose or (in the case of animals) is explained by beliefs and desires.

I have taken liberties in describing these plants. For dramatic effect I have spoken of these plants as having reasons for behaving the way they did. I described their behavior as purposive. The plants, of course, do not have reasons in the sense in which we have reasons. The plants do not have thoughts, desires, and intentions. They are not minded. Nonetheless, I used this way of speaking to make a point about the explanation of behavior. In explaining a system's behavior, we are often looking, not inside for the physical cause (C) of external change (E)—*that* is the business of chemistry (in the case of plants) and neurobiology (in the case of animals)—but outside for the events and circumstances that shaped internal structures, that made C cause E. We are looking for what I elsewhere (Dretske 1988) called *structuring*, not *triggering*, causes of behavior—the cause, not of E, but of C's causing E.

A bell rings and a classically conditioned dog behaves the way it was conditioned to behave: it salivates. Perhaps, given the conditioning process,the dog cannot help salivating when it hears the bell. The behavior, though not voluntary, *is* behavior, and we can seek an explanation for it. The bell rings (R), and this produces a certain auditory experience (E) in the dog. The dog hears the bell ring. These sensory events, as a result of conditioning, cause saliva to be secreted in the dog's mouth (M). What, then, causes the dog to salivate? Well, in one sense, the ringing bell causes the dog to salivate. At least the bell, by causing the dog to have a certain auditory experience, triggers a process that results in saliva's being secreted into the dog's mouth. The ringing bell is the triggering cause of behavior. Yes, but that doesn't tell us why the dog is doing what it is doing—only why it is doing it *now*. What we want to know is why the dog is salivating. Why isn't it, say, jumping? Other (differently trained) dogs jump when they hear the bell. Some (not trained at all) don't do much of anything. So why is this dog salivating? Why is it behaving this way? This, clearly, is a request, not for a triggering cause of the dog's behavior, but for a structuring cause. It is a request for the cause of one thing causing another, an explanation for why the auditory experience causes salivary glands to secrete. It doesn't do so in other dogs. Why? And once again, it seems the answer to this question lies in the past, in what learning theorists describe as the contingencies (correlations between the ringing bell and the arrival of food) to which the dog was exposed during training. If salivation is thought of as something the dog does (not simply as a glandular event occurring *to* the dog or *in* the dog)—if, in other words, it is thought of as behavior—then the causal explanation for it resides, not in the stimulus that elicits the behavior, but in facts about the dog's past experience.[19] Dog and Twin Dog might have much different reasons for salivating just as Scarlet Gilia and Twin Plant had much different reasons for changing color.

A question about the causal efficacy of the mental depends critically, therefore, on what the mental is supposed to causally explain. If thoughts, desires, and experiences are supposed to explain bodily movements and changes, events like the secretion of saliva in a dog's mouth, then it is, admittedly, hard to see how there could be different causes for the behavior of physically indistinguishable animals—how, for example, Dog and Twin Dog could have different reasons for salivating. The internal cause of glandular activity, the neurophysiological processes, would be the same in both. But if what the mental is asked to explain is not why saliva is being secreted in the dog's mouth, but why, when the dog hears a bell, it salivates, then it is easy to imagine Dog and Twin Dog salivating for much different reasons. And, for exactly the same reasons, it is easy to imagine Fred and Twin Fred moving their arms with much different purposes.[20]

Whether or not the mental has to supervene on the physical constitution of a system in order to be causally relevant to that system's behavior depends, therefore, on what one takes to be the behavior of the system. If behavior is identified, not with bodily movements and change, but with the causal processes that result in bodily movement and change, then the mental need not supervene in order to be causally relevant. On the contrary, if this is what behavior is, if this is what the mental is supposed to explain, one would expect the content of thought and the quality of experience to supervene not on the physical constitution of the animal but on the historical events and processes that shaped that animal's current control circuits—exactly where the Representational Thesis says it supervenes.

4   Evolutionary Origins

The Representational Thesis identifies conscious states with representational states, states that have a certain information-providing function. In the case of perceptual experiences, this function is systemic—derived from the perceptual system the states are states *of*. A state is a conscious experience of F (thus making its possessor sensuously aware of F) if the state has the natural (systemic) function of providing information about the F-ness of objects standing in the appropriate contextual relation (C) to the system. States thus become conscious by acquiring, for some determinable property F, the function of indicating, for appropriately related objects, their determinate value of F. Since states acquire their systemic functions through an evolutionary process—here assumed to be natural selection—natural selection is being identified as the source and creator of conscious experience.

It will surely be objected that natural selection does not create anything. It merely selects among traits that are—in one form or another—already present. If individual giraffes enjoy a competitive edge by having longer necks, then we can expect to see more giraffes with longer necks in succeeding generations. And if the advantage persists over many generations, and each generation comes with its stray longer-than-average-necks, natural selection can produce, over many generations, very long necks indeed. But natural selection does not, in any generation, make necks longer. Rather, in each succeeding generation, it makes more long necks (i.e., increases the proportion of longer necks).

Natural selection is not the creator of long necks. Instead, it uses long necks as the raw material out of which to make more of them. Consciousness is no different. If it is given a few to start with, natural selection can increase the number of conscious beings in succeeding generations. If someone is conscious, it can, as it were, make everyone conscious. But it cannot make someone conscious. If nobody is conscious, even to a small degree, then nobody enjoys the advantage of being conscious. If nobody enjoys the advantage of being conscious, consciousness cannot be selected for. It cannot evolve. This is why natural selection cannot create conscious beings, why it cannot be the origin of consciousness. It cannot give creatures something their ancestors did not already have. If we want to know where consciousness comes from, we will have to look someplace else for it.

The objection misidentifies the role that the Representational Thesis assigns to natural selection. Natural selection is not supposed to select for consciousness. That is not how the story goes. It selects for something else, something that, by being selected, becomes consciousness. Consider, for example, the process by means of which a variable resistor becomes a volume control. I'm building an amplifier and I want a variable resistor to use as a volume control. In my trip to the electronic parts store, I do not look at volume controls. I'm not selecting among volume controls. I am selecting among variable resistors, electrical components that are not yet (though they may become) volume controls. Once I have made my choice, once I have chosen a variable resistor and installed it in my amplifier, it becomes a volume control. But the fact that it, upon selection, becomes a volume control, does not mean that it started life that way, that it was, in some small way, already a volume control. Selection makes something a volume control. Given the right raw material, it can create volume controls. We don't have to start with volume controls in order to understand how, through this process of selection, they came into being.

Nor do we have to start with consciousness to understand how, through a process of natural selection, it comes into being. What natural selection starts with as raw material are organisms with assorted needs and variable resources for satisfying these needs. You don't have to be conscious to have needs. Even plants have needs. They need sunlight and water. An animal has a need for N if N is what it has to have to survive and reproduce. For creatures capable of behaving in need-satisfying ways, then, the benefits of information are clear. Information about external (and internal) affairs is necessary in order to coordinate behavior with the circumstances in which it has need-fulfilling consequences. No point in hiding if nothing is chasing. No point in chasing if there is nothing to catch. What natural selection does with this raw material is to develop and harness information-carrying systems to the effector mechanisms capable of using information to satisfy needs by appropriately directed and timed behavior. Once an indicator system is selected to provide the needed information it has the function of providing it. The states these systems produce by way of performing their informational duties then become representations of the conditions they have the (systemic) function of informing about. As a result, the organisms in which these states occur are aware of the objects and properties their internal representations represent. They see, hear, and smell things. Through a process of selection they have become perceptually conscious of what is going on around them.[21]

A word of caution. Despite my practice, throughout these lectures, of comparing (for illustrative purposes) natural and conventional functions and, therefore, natural and conventional representations, it is of the utmost importance for understanding this account of the origin of perceptual consciousness that one not confuse artificial selection with natural selection. The reason it is important to keep these processes distinct is that artificial selection can occur, but natural selection cannot, in the complete absence of any effective performance on the part of the item being selected. I can, for example, choose (or design) something to be a volume control (thus giving it that function) even when it is utterly incapable of controlling volume. Through ignorance or carelessness, I can select a variable capacitor to be my volume control, wire it to my amplifier, and wonder why it won't do the job I gave it. Artificial selection and conscious design are function-conferring activities that do not depend on objects *being able* to do what they are designed or selected to do. This is why it is possible to have conventional representations that are incapable of doing their job—incapable of indicating, even under optimal conditions, what they have the function of indicating. Such are the consequences of bad design, faulty manufacture and installation, and stupid choices.

Natural selection is quite different. Unlike artificial selection, an item cannot be naturally selected to do X unless it[22] actually does X. It has to do X because the way it gets selected is by having its performance of X contribute in some way to the survival and reproductive success of the animals in which it occurs. It is this contribution to reproductive success that, when it is selected for, confers a function on a system, and the function it confers is doing what the system *did* (in this case, provided information) that increased fitness. If a system didn't actually deliver information, its delivery of information could not have been selected for.[23] It could not, therefore, have acquired the function of delivering information. For a variable resistor to evolve, in some natural way, into a volume control, for natural selection to create a volume control, the resistor (i.e., some ancestral token of this resistor type) would actually have had to control volume. *I* can select a component to do a job that it cannot do, but nature cannot. Once a type of device has the function of controlling volume, current tokens of it need not—ever again!—control volume to retain their function. But it could not have acquired that function in any natural way unless it (i.e., earlier instantiations of it) actually did the job that it (i.e., later instantiations of it) have the function of performing.

For an information-delivery system to acquire the natural function of delivering information, for it to produce natural representations, then, the information it delivers must actually *do* something. It must make a positive causal contribution to fitness. It must be useful to, and actually used by (or have been used by), the organisms to which it is delivered. If it isn't, there can be no selection for the system that provides this information. We can build a system that doesn't *do* anything with the information it has the (conventional) function of delivering (measuring instruments are like this), but nature cannot. If nothing useful is done with the information, nothing in nature can acquire the function of providing it.[24]

As an act of blatant nepotism, I can hire my shiftless cousin, Wally, to perform a useless information-gathering task. I can pay him to keep track of the number of flies that land on my desk each day. Wally thereby has an information-collecting job. It is a conventional job, a job I give him. There are no natural jobs of this sort. There is nothing in nature capable of giving anyone, or anything, a job like this. This is why there are no Wally-senses or Wally-experiences, nothing in nature that has the function of supplying useless information.[25] There are none because it is only *by* supplying information the organism needs—or finds useful—that a system acquires the function of supplying it.

It is for this reason that gauges and instruments are not good analogies for sensory representations. Gauges and instrument do not *do* anything with the information they provide. Even if we could imagine automobiles reproducing and transmitting genetic material to their vehicular offspring, it would be hard to see why they would evolve into their present form. What would their gauges and instruments be for? Since these gauges perform no useful chores for the automobile, there would be no need for this information. Only if the information these instruments supplied was used in some way—to shift gears or apply the brakes—behaviors that contributed in some way to the reproductive success of the car—could we imagine these "sensors" being selected *for* and, thus, developing the function of supplying information to the car. Only then would the car start sensing its own speed, oil pressure, and gas level.

Since things acquire their functions gradually, over many generations, does this mean that consciousness comes in degrees? Does it mean that creatures gradually become conscious? Yes and No. Whether the answer is "yes" or "no" depends on whether one is talking about types or tokens, kinds or individuals. Yes, the process by means of which we—humans—became conscious is a gradual process. It did not—it cannot—happen overnight. I am conscious though I have distant ancestors who were not, and the evolutionary process responsible for this change is a gradual, a step-by-step, process. At the token, the individual, level, though, the answer is No. Individual human beings—you and I—do not become conscious in some gradual way. There is, of course, a sense in which we speak of ourselves as more or less conscious, of slowly regaining consciousness, of gradually losing consciousness, and so on, but our status as conscious beings, our capacity to be conscious, is not a status or capacity we come by gradually. In this (dispositional) sense, individuals are either conscious or they are not. It's like being pregnant.

But if I am conscious and my very distant ancestors were not, *when* did my less-distant ancestors start being conscious? At the same time a poor man becomes rich as you keep giving him pennies.

Notes

Prologue

1. I learned from Jerry Fodor that this simple phrase has the wondrous effect of discouraging troublesome quibbles.

Chapter 1

1. States also have indicator (information-providing) functions. For the present I concentrate on systems. In speaking of information and indication I draw heavily on Dretske 1981, 1988. The present account of representation, minus some important refinements (particularly the distinction between experience and thought), is to be found in Dretske 1986, 1988. Though I rely on my earlier work, I have tried to make the present account self-contained.

2. Hereafter I will omit the "mere." In speaking of facts about representations, therefore, I should be understood as meaning facts about representations that are not also representational facts.

3. I think that natural selection is not the only source of natural functions. Learning is also a source. This was the basis of my (Dretske 1988) account of belief. I return to this point shortly when I distinguish representational states whose indicator functions are *systemic* (phylogenetic) from representational states whose functions are acquired during individual learning (ontogenetic).

4. I happen to favor the account of biological functions described by Godfrey-Smith (1994)—see also Kitcher 1993—as "the modern history theory of functions." The present account, however, is independent of one's

particular theory of natural functions or where, exactly, they come from. It may even turn out, as Tim Schroeder has suggested to me, that maturational processes in the individual can be the source of functions for a developing perceptual system as it establishes its anatomical connections in and to the brain. As long as there are natural functions—whatever the correct understanding of them might be—that is enough for my naturalistic project. I will, however, assume in this work that natural functions are always acquired through some historical process like natural selection (for systems) and learning (for states). I return to this topic, and the problems it creates for a representational theory of experience, in chapter 5.

5. I shall, of course, have much more to say about just *why*, and in what sense, this is so. See Rey 1988 for scepticism about this way of distinguishing biological from artifactual systems.

6. Not all natural systems of representation are mental. There are, for example, homeostatic and other regulative mechanisms that depend on "sensors" whose biological function is to indicate such things as glucose levels in the blood, temperature in the hypothalamus, and so on. If this is, indeed, the biological function of these sensors, then there are, in the sense defined here, natural representations in the autonomic nervous system that are in no way mental. At least they are not conscious. The Representational Thesis does not deny this. It says that all mental facts are representational, not that all representations, not even all *natural* representations, are mental.

7. It is not enough to have the retina (ear drum) stimulated by light (sound) from the piano. Not even enough to have these signals relayed to the cortex. Unless an experience occurs, as it won't if there is (say) massive damage to the brain, nothing is seen or heard.

8. Most philosophers acknowledge a sharp distinction between thought (judgment, belief, etc.) and sensation (experience) although they differ on what, ultimately, this distinction comes down to. Some (e.g., Armstrong 1969; Dennett 1969, 1991; Pitcher 1971) try to analyze experience in cognitive terms, as "suppressed," "potential," "micro," or otherwise unconscious judgments that things are (or seem) a certain way. Others (e.g., Block 1994; Crane 1992; Davies 1992; Dretske 1969, 1981, 1993; Evans 1982; Jackendoff 1987; McGinn 1989; Millar 1992; Peacocke 1992; and Perkins 1983, to name only a few) make a clear separation of conceptual and sensory affairs. Smelling burning toast is *not* a type of belief or judgment. Unlike a belief or judgment, it does not require the concepts (on the part of the animal doing the smelling) used in expressing what one is aware of. The distinction between an experience of an F and a belief that it is an F is what (in Dretske 1990, 1993) I called the difference between thing-awareness and fact-awareness and what (in Dretske 1969) I described as the difference between non-

epistemic (hearing a piano being played) and epistemic perception (hearing that a piano is being played). Block's (1990b, 1993) distinction between phenomenal and access consciousness is, I think, another way of describing this difference.

Although the language used to describe the differences serves different purposes, the same distinctions are evident in cognitive psychology. Instead of the word "experience," one finds the same phenomena described in terms of percepts, early levels of representation (e.g., Marr 1982), *precategorical* representations of sensory attributes (van der Heijden 1992), *iconic* and *echoic* information stores (Neisser 1967; Eysenck 1990), *sensory registers* (Shiffrin and Atkinson 1969), *feature buffers* (Mewhort et al. 1981), and so on. Using Marr's terminology, Jackendoff (1989, p. 294) describes visual awareness (a preconceptual mode of awareness) as determined by the 2 1/2 D sketch, whereas visual understanding (what he describes as the "content" or "meaning" of visual awareness) is determined by the 3D sketch and related conceptual structures. Humphrey (1992, p. 44) contrasts two kinds of representation—one that leads to the "qualia of subjective feelings" (what I am calling experience) and the other "to the intentional objects of cognition and objective knowledge" (what is believed or known).

9. I take this to be a conversational implicature, not a logical or conceptual implication, but it makes no difference for my purposes which it is. The potential for confusion is the same.

10. For a long time it was thought that cats lacked color vision because they did not discriminate colors behaviorally. It is now known, however, that cats *perceptually* discriminate colors. They *perceive* colors. They have color *vision*. Without special training, though, they do not respond to the perceived differences. For the difference between behavioral and perceptual discrimination, see Geoffrey Hall's article on "Discrimination" in McFarland (1987).

11. As Godfrey-Smith (1989, pp. 542–543) points out, it is systems (for producing states), not the states these systems produce, that are subject to the process of natural selection.

12. Although individual developmental differences cannot affect what an experience represents$_s$, they can change what an experience represents$_a$. I am not denying that learning can change the way things looks, sound, and feel. When we describe how things look, sound and feel, we are often describing a combination of both sensory and conceptual appearances. I return to these issues in chapters 3 and 5.

13. In talking about conventional representations, the subscript "a" on both functions and representations can be read "assigned."

14. We could even imagine assigning a 60 mph function to a state that had the systemic function of indicating 50 mph. This might be desirable if the instrument, through some defect in manufacture, regularly registered too low. This is a version of the inverted spectrum problem—sensing redly but believing greenly—and I will return to it in chapter 3.

15. We will see in chapter 5, §4, why experiences *must* make the information they supply available (via a cognitive system) to control mechanisms. That is the only way they can acquire the function of supplying it.

16. In Dretske 1981 I described the relationship between sensation and cognition in terms of the way information is encoded. In these terms, the condition an analog representation must satisfy to qualify as a experience is that the information it has the function of providing must be available for digitalization (i.e., conceptual treatment). Conceptual processes, in turn, are simply those involved in the construction and use of representations$_a$—the representations that (together with desires) are used in the control and regulation of behavior.

17. Thus, food *specialists* (McFarland 1981, p. 210)—blowflies, frogs, tapeworms, etc.—those creatures who have separate detector systems for each nutrient they need and inflexible (not susceptible to change by learning) responses to each, have, on this account, no experience of the food their detectors detect. Since they have no cognitive system for the detectors to service, no way of recalibrating in terms of individual needs and circumstances, their representations of food do not qualify as experiences of food. Food *generalists* (ibid.), on the other hand, those organisms (like us) who do not have food recognition mechanisms built in genetically, must learn through experience what is food and what is not. In our case, the representationss of food qualify as experiences of food, and they do so even before we have learned that it is food we are experiencing.

18. See Peacocke's (1983) discussion of "sensational" properties and his later (1992b) notion of "protopropositional" content for considerations that strongly suggest the need for distinguishing between two sorts of properties of perceptual experience. See, also, Millar 1991, pp. 470–452.

19. I am indebted to Berent Enc, Peter Godfrey-Smith, David Hilbert, Mohan Matthen, Dennis Stampe, and Tim Schroeder for useful discussion of the material in this section.

20. If we include (as I do) the properties a representation represents (the *way* it depicts what—if anything—it depicts) as (part) of what it is *of* or *about*, then a representation (hence, experience) will always be *of* or *about* something. When there is no object (e.g., a round square) the experience will be of or about the properties (roundness and squareness) it (mis)represents an object to have. See below for this type of misrepresentation.

21. I will not here try to say what this external relation C is (see Evans 1982; McDowell 1986; Recanati 1993, p. 116, n. 9). It is obviously more than a simple causal relation. Many things stand in a causal relation to a representation (such as an experience) that are not the objects of that representation (not the object we experience). In Dretske 1981, pp. 153–168, I attempted to fix this relation in terms of the informational relations between perceiver and object. I still think this account comes close. See Perkins 1983, pp. 99–101, 244, and passim, for insightful discussions of the problems in specifying a perceptual object for the various senses. Is it, for example, air temperature or skin temperature (or neither) we feel when we feel "it" getting hotter?

22. According to Christensen (1993, p. 760) this is why Husserl says that our perception of things is "objective" or "transcends consciousness": the object perceived need not be as perceived nor need it be at all.

23. There is a difference in the aspectual features of experience and thought, but I pass over these complications here. I also pass over questions of whether a representational story (when told in terms of indicator functions) is enough to "slice" the aspects finely enough. Can it, for instance, distinguish between the representation of k as F and the representation of k as G when F and G are necessarily (nomically, logically, or metaphysically) equivalent properties? I think it can, but to appreciate the problems, see Fodor (1994).

Chapter 2

1. For a similar view of introspection, see Shoemaker 1986, 1994, and Evans 1982, especially pp. 224–235.

2. By "external" and "internal" ("outside" and "inside") I mean, of course, external (internal) to *the mind* (not the body) As I am using the term, feeling a broken tooth with your tongue is perceiving an external object. The endoscope (medical instrument for viewing internal organs) is not a useful *introspective* device. Humphrey (1992, p. 97) describes a person who could hear himself "see"; at least he could hear blood rushing to his visual cortex when he opened his eyes and saw objects. Though this might count as perception of internal events and processes, it does not, on present usage, count as introspection.

3. The *target* fact—that k is F—is displaced. The epistemically intermediate fact—that h is G—is not. In Dretske (1969) I called this "secondary" (epistemic) perception.

4. This isn't quite right, but it will do for my purposes. One *may* perceive k when seeing, by h's being G, that k is F. The point is that it is the way h appears, not the way k appears, that tells you that k is F. Seeing that the cake is done by looking at the toothpick I extract from it counts as displaced perception even if I happen to also see the cake.

5. There will normally also be a conceptual representation of the properties of the scale (e.g., its pointer position) that "tells" one how much one weighs. To see that one weighs 178 pounds, it is not enough to see the pointer pointing at "178." One has to see *that* it is pointing at "178."

6. I ignore these epistemological niceties. Some philosophers, of course, would deny that one could come to know that k was F by seeing that h was G merely by *assuming* (without justification or knowledge) that h would not be G unless k were (probably) F.

7. It is not clear how or whether pictures (pictorial representations) can do this—whether, that is, the picturing relation is picturable (see Perner 1991). A picture of both Clyde and a picture of Clyde—a picture of Clyde standing next to his portrait, say—does not picture the portrait as being a portrait of Clyde. It could be a picture of Clyde standing next to a portrait of his twin brother. Or it could be a picture of Clyde and his twin brother with the latter standing inside a frame (hence, not even a picture of a representation at all).

8. I assume that knowledge—involving belief—is always conceptual.

9. To model our knowledge of a person's (hence, our own) *sensory* states, I will be concerned with the systemic representational properties of the gauge, what its pointer positions represent$_s$ about k.

10. To be carefully distinguished (see chapter 1, §4) from there being something it represents to be 14 psi.

11. We could, of course, raise questions about how we know it is a pressure gauge instead of an altimeter, a badly designed wind gauge, or something having no indicator function whatsoever. These are good questions, and I return to them below and in chapter 3, §5.

12. Unless, as with commercial instruments, someone (e.g., the manufacturer) "tells" you by printing words or other function-revealing symbols there.

13. Matthen (1988, p. 13) rightly points out that there are (what he calls) "normal misperceptions." These are misrepresentations that are part of the normal functioning of the system, results that occur because imperfect mechanisms (the best available at the time) were selected to perform the

indicator functions. Though they are working properly—as best they can—they sometimes register F to have a value it does not have. Normal speedometers (the pointer positions of which are calibrated at the factory) misrepresent the speed of the car when under-sized tires are used. That isn't the fault of the speedometer. It is working as well as it can, the way it was designed to work. This is, in Matthen's sense, a normal misrepresentation. Likewise, subjective contours (Kanizsa 1976), apparent motion (Ramachandran and Anstis 1986), Benham's Top (a device for pulsing white light to produce experiences of other colors; Gregory 1987, pp. 78–79) and a host of other sensory "illusions" testify to the power of the senses to misrepresent when they are functioning normally.

This point is correct, as far as it goes, and I will return to it in chapter 3, §5, when I discuss the source of natural functions and how a mechanism can have the function of indicating F when there are circumstances in which, without malfunctioning, it will misrepresent F. For the present, I simply note that when I speak of a system functioning properly, working as it was designed to work, I mean to include its being connected (by the appropriate C relations) to the objects whose F it is designed to indicate. Using a (precalibrated) speedometer in a car with undersized tires is not connecting the instrument to the kind of object whose speed it has the function of indicating. It has the function of indicating the speed of cars with normal-sized tires. *That*, obviously, is why it was calibrated the way it was. Using it in circumstances in which it was not designed to function is not allowing it to work according to design. Likewise, staring at flashing monochromatic sodium yellow light (and experiencing pink) or observing rapidly alternating spots (as apparent motion) is not (I conjecture) using the visual system's color and movement detectors in conditions they were designed to function. Whether they were designed to function in these unusual circumstances depends on the selectional history of the systems (see chapter 3, §5).

14. Davidson (1987) also has a well-known response to such criticisms, but since the present (representational) version of externalism is much closer to the Burge-Heil defense than it is to Davidson's, I concentrate on Burge and Heil. For versions of the Burge-Heil position see, also, Shoemaker 1994, p. 260 and n. 7; Lepore and Loewer 1986; Evans 1982, p. 204; Davidson 1988. p. 664; Noonan 1993; Wright 1991; and Stalnaker 1990. For a critique of the Burge-Heil position, see Bilgrami 1992.

15. Burge acknowledged this in a recent (November 1994) conversation. This is all he took himself to be showing.

16. This fact gives rise to a failure of closure for perceptual knowledge. Despite knowing that nothing can be a tomato without being a physical

object, S can, for instance, see that *k* is a tomato without *seeing* (without even being *able* to *see*—though, of course, S may know) that *k* is a physical object. In Dretske 1969 I called the knowledge presupposed in such perceptual claims (knowledge that the object seen to be a tomato is a physical object) "protoknowledge." Closure also fails—and for the same reason—in the case of introspective knowledge: S can know, by introspection, that it is F she is experiencing without knowing, without being able to know, *by introspection*, that she is experiencing F. She can know, by introspection, *what* is in the mind, but not *that* it is in a mind.

17. I am indebted to Sven Bernecker, a stubborn and insightful sceptic, for helpful discussion on the matter of what we can and cannot know by introspection. See Bernecker (forthcoming).

18. Evans (1982, pp. 224–235) makes the same point: introspective knowledge of experience requires not just information about experience but the concept of experience. He gives an example that is particularly apt. A person (and any other animal who has eyes in the front) seeing a tree is getting information about herself—that she is *facing* the tree. That doesn't mean she knows or believes it.

19. Quinton (1977) makes a similar point: what makes the knowledge noninferential is not that there is no inference, but that the inference is infallible.

20. This point has been made by a variety of philosophers and psychologists. See, for example, Dennett 1991a; Harman 1990; Hebb 1969; Lyons 1986, p. 96; McGinn 1982a; Rosenthal 1990, 1991a; Shoemaker 1986, 1994; Tye 1992.

Chapter 3

1. This definition is not circular. The primitive terms are look-the-same and look-different. Looking$_p$ like F is defined as looking the same as Fs normally look (and different from a certain range of non-Fs). It is similar to defining various lengths (1 meter, 10 meters) in terms of being as-long-as and ten times longer-than other (standard) objects.

2. Which isn't to say they never are. One can imagine trying to distinguish real French poodles from fakes. In this context, saying that a dog looks like a French poodle implies one *can* discriminate it from a fake.

3. I think my distinction between appearances$_p$ and appearances$_d$ is close to Millar's (1991) distinction between F-type experiences (phenomenal) and seemings-that-F-is-there (doxastic). Also Peacocke 1983. Churchland's

(1979, p. 14) distinction between subjective and objective intentionality is similar.

4. See Lloyd 1989, chapter 5, for a summary of relevant data from Lettvin et al. 1959 to Ewart 1987.

5. Notice, if I am confused enough, I may be caused to believe that it is a red Burgundy. The wine may, that is, taste$_d$ like a red Burgundy to me.

6. Even aside from the problems to be mentioned in a moment, there are technical difficulties in using perceptual discrimination as a criteria for what properties a sensory system represents. Clark (1993, p. 59) points out that the indiscriminability of two stimuli does not suffice to show that they present the observer with identical qualia. If there is some Qi which is indiscriminable from Q1 but not from Q2, then, despite the indiscriminability of Q1 from Q2, they must be "presented" (i.e., represented) differently. The failure of a system to discriminate "locally" between two conditions is not enough, therefore, to show that the system is representing the two conditions as the same. What is needed is what Clark calls "global" indiscriminability. I skip over these complications here. They do not affect the point I will be making.

7. I give the "inverted spectrum" problem this slightly novel twist to avoid objections to standard formulations. Hardin (1988) and van Gulick (1993, pp. 144–145), for example, contend that most inversions imagined by philosophers would disrupt the organization of highly structured quality spaces, and, therefore, have detectable effects (i.e., contribute to differences in discriminatory powers). In the cases I am imagining, there is very little, if any, quality space left to be disrupted.

8. Rey (1992, pp. 59–61) and Lycan (1987, p. 297) argue that there is a deep difference in the way the problem of inverted qualia arise for behaviorists and functionalists.

9. This benefit of a representational theory has been appreciated by Harman (1990), Tye (1991, 1992, 1994), Davies (1991), Lycan (1987, 1990), McGinn (1991). Though I would classify all these philosophers as "representationalists" (Shoemaker [1990b] calls them "intentionalists"), not many would endorse my *naturalistic* version of representationalism and few would agree that *all* introspectively accessible qualities are intentional (i.e., represented properties). See Shoemaker 1994, p. 22.

10. E.g., Shoemaker (1975, 1991). But see Lycan 1987, p. 60: "The possibility of spectrum inverted with respect to i-o [input-ouput] relations alone is a well-entrenched and respectable though I suppose defeasible modal intuition; the possibility of spectrum inverted with respect to i-o relations *plus*

internal functional organization at however low a level of abstraction proponents feel it plausible to name is anything but obvious and in conflict with some intuitively plausible supervenience theses." I take up problems about supervenience in chapter 5.

11. I ignore distracting complications about "coded" rings; e.g., only uncle Clyde plays Yankee Doodle Dandy when he rings the bell. I also ignore the possibility of doorbells rung by woodpeckers, pesky squirrels, etc.

12. Damasio and Damasio (1993, p. 57) point out that damage to certain parts of the brain causes, not only the loss of color perception (achromatopsia), but loss of an ability to imagine colors. Damage to other portions of the brain, and to early stages of visual processing, do not result in similar defects. One can still imagine colors even though one cannot see them. In some sense, they conclude, the concept of color (I would say the power to represent color) depends on this region of the brain. I am imagining Susan with this part of the brain operational. What is damaged is some part of the visual system responsible for delivering information about color to this part of the brain.

13. It is important to recall that a system might represent (i.e, have the function of providing information about) properties that were not originally of any particular "interest" to the system. See the distinction between explicit and "implied" indicator functions in chapter 1, §3.

14. Actually, it means something more like not-77.5 (and below) and not-78.5 (and above), but the point, I hope, is clear enough without these fussy details.

15. Biro (1991, p. 121) also argues—convincingly, it seems to me—that there is nothing particularly mental about *portable* points of view (those points of view we cannot exchange with each other) if their portability is simply a trivial consequence of their being *our* point of view the way my haircuts are necessarily my haircuts and, thus, different from yours. Even the simplest instruments have a unique point of view in this (portable) sense: how this thermometer represents the temperature in X differs from how that thermometer represents the temperature in X (even if they both represent it as 98°) because this thermometer is not that thermometer.

16. This is pretty simple, probably *too* simple to be very realistic. Even ticks have a sensory system that responds to three stimuli: (1) diffuse light (they have no eyes); (2) the smell of butyric acid; and (3) heat. See McFarland 1987, p. 449.

17. Since these are just examples, I will not worry here about whether dogfish and parasites have experiences. I said earlier (chapter 1, §3) that for a

representation$_s$ to be an experience, it must service a representational$_a$ (conceptual) system, a system that can, through learning, recalibrate the informational functions of its indicator states. I'm not going to worry whether this condition is satisfied in the case of dogfish and parasites.

18. Given my choice of examples, it may be worth noting that mosquitoes (Grier 1984, p. 447) have been reported to be sensitive to as small a temperature difference as .002°C and fish to as small a difference as .02°C. Furthermore, some animals have "absolute pitch" with respect to these quantities. Rodents, bees, and fish can be trained to choose a particular temperature that does not depend on a relative difference with previous temperature.

19. Or so Georges Rey (in correspondence) tells me. Actually, I think George didn't put it this delicately. He said something closer to, "It *is* preposterous." I prefer the first way of putting it since, as I will try to show, the appearances are deceptive.

20. Which is *not* the same as knowing what it is like to see a square. In seeing a square many more properties than 4-sidedness are being represented, and one may not know these other properties. I return to this point in §5.

21. Clark (1993, p. 206) describes a similar pattern of discrimination tests as revealing (in the case of the bat) an answer ("of sorts") to the question, What is it like to be a bat? We get, he says (207), "what seems to be" an "objective" characterization of what it is like to be a bat. The only respects in which Clark and I differ is that a teleological view of representation makes the qualifiers ("of sorts" and "what seems to be") unnecessary.

22. Many philosophers have made this point in response to Jackson's argument—the point that there are no facts Mary cannot know (about the experience of other creatures) unless facts are so finely individuated that my knowledge that this (the only thing I see) is green and your knowledge that what I see is green count as knowledge of different facts. See Davies and Humphrey 1993, pp. 16–17; Evans 1984; Horgan 1984; Loar 1990; Lycan 1990; Papineau 1993; Rey 1993; Shoemaker 1991, p. 508; Tye 1986; and Van Gulick 1993, p. 142.

23. See Thompson et al. 1992 for a useful survey of current positions.

24. Compare Colin McGinn's (1989, pp. 77–78) example of a pattern recognition device that consistently "misinterprets" the stimulus in a novel environment.

26. For what it is worth, Meltzoff and Borton (1979) give evidence of intersensory equivalence in neonates. One-month-olds were familiarized to one of two dummies (pacifiers) placed in their mouths. One dummy had a

smooth nipple while the other, nubby nipple, had protuberances on it. Following familiarization the babies were shown visual replicas of the two dummies and they showed a reliable visual preference for the one they had previously perceived orally. (Taken from Eysenck 1990, p. 261).

Chapter 4

1. Idealists, Moore claimed, confused what we experience (which may or may not be mental) with our experience of it (which certainly is mental). The result? That everything we are aware of is mental.

2. I here ignore dispositional senses of the relevant terms—the sense in which we say of someone or something that it is a conscious being even if, at the time we describe it this way, it is not (in an occurrent sense) conscious. So, for example, in the dispositional sense, I am a conscious being even during dreamless sleep.

3. David Rosenthal has pointed out to me that even if I use the terms "conscious" and "aware" as synonyms, conscious awareness is not necessarily a redundancy. Being consciously aware of something may mean being conscious *that* you are aware of it, something that is not implied in your being aware of it. This is certainly correct. When I have the Rosenthal reading in mind, I will always make it explicit.

4. I here ignore disputes about whether, in some strict sense, we are really aware of the person or only (in smell) an odor emanating from the person or (in hearing) his or her voice or the noise they make. I shall always take the perceptual object (if there is one) to be a physical object or condition, but I will not be concerned with just *what* object or condition this is. This is, I assume, an empirical issue; the answer depends on what properties the representation has the function of providing information about (see chapter 1, §4). Perkins (1983) has a nice discussion of the problems (for realists like me) in specifying the perceptual object.

5. I assume that a sense-data analysis of dreams and hallucination is false. I assume, that is, that when a person hallucinates pink rats, the person is not aware of any *object* that is pink and rat-shaped. This is not to deny that the person is aware of certain *properties* (pinkness, etc.), the same properties, in fact, that a person seeing a pink rat is aware of. It is only to say that he is not aware of any *object* that has these properties—anything that *is* pink and rat-shaped.

6. In the case of dreams, this means that the dreamer, though unconscious in one sense, is (while dreaming) conscious in another. Compare

Nikolnakos (1994, p. 96), who suggests that for these reasons dreamers are conscious while in the REM state.

7. I would, that is, say many of the same things (but certainly not *all* the same things) about them as Armstrong (1968), Pitcher (1970), and Michael Tye (1991, 1992, 1994, and forthcoming) say. In particular, pain (thirst, an itch, etc.) is not a sensation, a mental particular, one is aware of. It is not an *object* of awareness. It is, rather, an *awareness* of an object—a bodily state.

8. HO theories are theories of *state* consciousness—of what makes a state a conscious state. They are not theories of consciousness. These theories have nothing to say (at least I have seen nothing) about what constitutes *creature* consciousness of lower-order states.

9. I leave out the "if" since HO theories typically want to add that this higher order awareness must be appropriately "noninferential" in order to make the lower order experience conscious. Coming to believe (and, thus, becoming aware) that one hates one's father by being told this by a psychoanalyst, for example, is not to make the hatred conscious. The higher-order belief (that one has such a hatred) is not suitably *direct*. I ignore this aspect of HO theories since my criticism of HO theories will not turn on this feature.

10. I say "perhaps" because Armstrong has a view about perception (as the having or acquiring of beliefs) that blurs the distinction between thought and experience—thus, between HOT and HOE theories. I am grateful to Güven Güzeldere for pointing this out to me.

11. I am grateful to Güven Güzeldere for helpful discussion on this point. See Güzeldere (forthcoming). After writing this lecture I read Sydney Shoemaker's (1994) critique of perceptual models of introspection. He makes many of the same criticisms that I make here and in chapter 2. Also see Evans 1982: ". . . there is no *informational* state [i.e., higher-order experience, FD] which stands to the internal state [the lower-order experience, FD] as that internal state stands to the state of the world" (228).

12. Via recently devised imaging techniques—e.g., PET (positron emission tomography) and MRI (magnetic resonance imaging).

13. The fact that we do not (ever!) remember seeing the moustache does not mean we did not see it—that we were not conscious of it. It simply means that we never became conscious *that* we were conscious *of* it (that we had an experience of it).

I also have in mind more exotic phenomena: e.g., split-brain patients who are (with the right side of their brain) conscious of various things (they see and feel things on the left) but do not appear to be aware (at least not with the left side of their brain—the language side) *that* they are aware of these things. See Milner 1992, p. 153; Rugg 1992, p. 275; and Young and De Haan 1990 for discussion (the latter describe the differences between this and blindsight). I should also mention so-called "iconic" memory (for this term see Neisser 1967) that I discussed in Dretske 1981. Sperling's (1960) and Averbach and Coriell's (1961) experiments with brief visual displays indicate that subjects see (and, hence, are conscious *of*) more than they can possibly identify or report on.

14. This is a much discussed topic of late; see e.g., Velmans 1991; Humphrey 1983; Rey 1988; Van Gulick 1989; and many others.

15. David Rosenthal points out to me that according to HOT, although E (some experience) doesn't acquire any additional causal powers by being conscious, there nonetheless may be a purpose served by E's being conscious. The purpose lies not in the beneficial effects of a conscious E (there is no difference in the effects of conscious and nonconscious Es), but in the effects of the higher-order thought that makes E conscious. This sounds right, but it should be noted that such a move would also give a function, some purpose, to conscious diseases. They are more quickly reported to the doctor, etc.

16. This is not to say that consciousness is *always* advantageous. As Georges Rey reminds me, some tasks—playing the piano, pronouncing language, and playing fast sports—are best performed when the agent is largely unaware of the details. Nonetheless, even here, consciousness of the more remote objective—the securing of which these details contribute to—is essential.

17. For more on blindsight see Weiskrantz 1986 and Milner and Rugg 1992. I here assume that the subject's (professed) absence of visual experience is tantamount to a claim that they cannot see objects, that they have no visual experience. The question that blindsight raises is why one has to see X (or anything else, for that matter) in order to see what (who, where, etc.) X is if those with blindsight can do it *without* seeing anything.

18. There are a good many reflexive "sensings" (Walker 1983, p. 240) that involve no awareness of the stimulus that is controlling behavior—e.g., accommodation of the lens of the eye to objects at different distances, reactions of the digestive system to internal forms of stimulation, direction of gaze toward peripherally seen objects. Milner (1992, p. 143) suggests that these "perceptions" are probably accomplished by the same midbrain visuomotor systems as mediate prey catching in frogs and orienting reactions in rats and monkeys. What is puzzling about blindsight is not that we get information we are not aware of (these reflexive sensings are all

instances of that), but that in the case of blindsight one appears able to use this information in the control and guidance of deliberate, intentional, action (when forced to do so)—the sort of action that normally requires awareness.

Chapter 5

1. E.g., in Davies 1991; Horgan 1991; Fodor 1980, 1987; McGinn 1989; Seager 1991; Sterelny 1990; Lloyd 1989; Tye (forthcoming); and many, many, others.

2. E.g., those involving natural kinds. I think, though, that convincing Twin Earth type arguments can be given for the view that *no* concept for which there is an appearance-reality distinction) is (wholly) in the head. Needless to say, this includes most concepts. See below (e.g., note 5).

3. It was, say, synthesized in the laboratory or materialized in the manner of Davidson's (1987) Swampman.

4. In Dretske 1981, 1988 I developed, and defended, an externalist theory of belief and desire.

5. In order to keep the focus clear, I will suppose that Twin Fred, after growing up in an alien environment, has been miraculously transported to Fred's habitat, and is looking at the same stuff: k. Differences in what they think about what they see will thus be determined *not* by a difference in the object they see (what their beliefs are beliefs about), but by what they believe about it—the conceptual content of their perceptual beliefs.

For the sake of exposition, I will also assume that flim and flam are distal properties (or kinds) of objects in Fred's and Twin Fred's respective environments. It makes no difference what kind of properties these are. They needn't be natural kinds. What is important to the argument is that flims be *external* in the sense that there are circumstances in which nonflims can be made to look exactly like flims—that nonflims can produce the same proximal input as flims. If this condition is met—and I do not see how anything *less* could be used to illustrate an externalist theory of thought—then it will be possible to construct a Twin-Earth type situation between Fred and Twin-Fred, a situation in which flims cause in Fred exactly the same physical condition that nonflims (e.g., flams) cause in Twin Fred. Thus, Fred and Twin Fred can be imagined to be in the same physical state while differing in what their thoughts are thoughts about.

6. I remind the reader about my use of subscripts (see chapter 3): the subscript "d" (standing for doxastic) signifies a sense of "look" ("appear," "seem," etc.) that implies something about the beliefs (or belief disposi-

tions) of the S to whom something looks$_d$ F. k looksd F to S = S believes (or—see chapter 3, §1 for details—would normally believe), on the basis of her perception of k, that k is F. The subscript "p" (for phenomenal), on the other hand, does not imply anything about the doxastic state or disposition of S—nothing, therefore, about S's conceptual resources. k looks$_p$ F to S = k looks the same (in certain F-ish respects) to S as Fs look (once again, see chapter 3, §1 for essential qualifications). A dog might look$_p$ like a French poodle to Susan even if she doesn't know what a French poodle is (it might, that is, cause in Susan an experience similar to ones that French poodles cause), but it couldn't look$_d$ like a French poodle to her if she didn't know what a French poodle was (if, that is, she did not take, or was not disposed to take, dogs that looked that way to be French poodles).

7. Kant said that without concepts, *intuitions* were blind. If we take intuitions to be experiences, it isn't the intuitions that are blind; it is by their means (by the fact that they occur in us) that we are made aware of (i.e., see and hear) the objects around us. It is, rather, the intuitions that we cannot be made aware of.

8. There are a variety of reasons why, though possessing the concept F, things might not look$_d$ F to S even though they look$_p$ F. Inattention is probably the most common reason: I *must* have seen the color of your tie (I looked straight at it several times), but I was so engrossed in our conversation that I didn't pay any attention. That is to say, your tie must have looked$_p$ blue to me but, because of inattention, it did not lookd blue to me (did not cause me to believe it was blue). Sensory overload is another: one sees more than one can possibly have beliefs about. For this possibility, Sperling's (1960) experiments with brief visual displays are suggestive: subjects *see* an array of numbers under very brief exposure conditions. They can identify, at most, three or four, but the fact that they can identify *any* three or four (which three or four they identify depends on later cueing) suggests that, at (or possibly at) the phenomenal level, there is information about *all* the letters. The unidentified "5"s look$_p$ like "5"s even though they do not look$_d$ like "5"s. There is also hypnosis, sleep walking, and damage or impairment to higher-level processing centers (I am thinking here of commissurotomy, various agnosias, and unilateral visual neglect).

9. Assuming that one (originally) saw all the fingers one (thereafter) counts. There is the possibility, of course, that, in counting the fingers, one sees (sequentially) more fingers than one (originally) saw (all at the same time). But, often enough, and despite Dan Dennett's (1991a) protests to the contrary, when the numbers are small it is entirely reasonable to suppose that one saw all of the fingers one counts. One just doesn't (without count-

ing) know how many one saw. As Farah (1990, p. 18) points out, counting *requires* seeing more than one object at a time. It seems clear that it also requires seeing more than one *knows* (though not necessarily more than one *thinks*) one is seeing. Why else would one count? See Perkins 1983 for helpful discussion on this point.

10. I avoid using subscripts for the moment in order to illustrate the ambiguity in normal conversations that my use of subscripts is designed to avoid.

11. There is a sense in which these are not the same. I might know enough musical theory to know what a change of key *is*, but not be able to *hear* it. If I know enough musical theory to know what a change of key is, but lack the capacity to identify changes of key auditorily, then it becomes possible for me to hear a change of key (it sounds$_p$ to me like a change of key), know what the property is that I am hearing, but not know (at least not by hearing) whether I am hearing it.

12. And this is *different* from what no change key sound like to me. It is important to add this qualification since, as we saw in chapter 3, nothing need sound$_p$ like a change of key to me just because it sounds the way changes of key normally sound to me. If I am virtually deaf and almost everything sounds the same to me, then changes of key are not part of my phenomenal experience. Nothing sounds$_p$ like a change of key to me even if it causes in me an experience just like those that key changes normally cause in me.

13. For present purposes I take zombies to be beings who lack thoughts and experiences but who are functionally (perhaps even physically) indistinguishable from minded creatures. Some materialists think that zombies are not possible. A representational theory of thought and experience of the present sort—indeed, any externalist theory of the mind—says that they are possible. There can be counterfeit thinkers (i.e., zombies) for the same reason there can be counterfeit $100 bills: the counterfeits are objects that do not stand in the right relations to other things. They do not, for instance, have the right history.

14. By "placement" I mean the way the parts function (their causes and effects) in the system (if any) of which they are a part. So Twin Tercel's parts not only look like Tercel's gauges, they (all but the gas gauge, that is) *function* in the same way (relaying information about speed, oil pressure, etc.). An historical view of functions is committed to the view that A and B can function in the same way without having the same function.

15. It would not be irrelevant if we accepted a Cummins (1975) style of analysis of functions according to which the function of a part is, roughly,

what it does to contribute to the capacities of a containing system. That this is *not* our intuitive understanding of functions is, I take it, obvious from the fact that we naturally judge Twin Tercel's gas gauge to be broken. It couldn't be broken on a Cummins understanding of functions since it doesn't, and never did, do anything.

16. William Paley (1743–1805), an English theologian and moral philosopher, advanced a well-known argument for the existence of God. If you found something as complex as a watch in the middle of a heath, would you not infer it had a designer? Paley argued that the care with which the parts have been made and the fineness of their adjustment can have only one implication: that the watch must have had a maker who understood its construction and who designed it for the use for which it is fitted. So, also, in the case of the exquisite contrivance of the human body. All this sounded much more plausible before Darwin, of course.

17. I do not wish to suggest that Horgan is disputing it. My clarificatory remarks are not aimed at Horgan. He is quite clear about the distinction between the here-and-now character of the belief (what I, in chapter 1, called the belief *vehicle*) and the here-and-now character of *what* is believed (the belief-*content*).

18. For details, see Dretske 1988, 1990b, 1991a, 1991b, 1992, 1993a, 1993b, 1994, and forthcoming.

19. I do not deny that we are *sometimes* looking for triggering causes of behavior. One need only imagine a deaf laboratory assistant, someone completely familiar with the dog's training history, asking why the dog is salivating. This person needs to be told something about the triggering cause. He needs to be told that the bell is ringing.

20. It has been objected by Baker (1991) and others that what structuring causes explain is not the individual behaviors that beliefs and desires explain, but certain behavioral *dispositions*—why, for example, the dog is disposed to salivate when the bell rings. As I point out in my reply to Baker (Dretske 1991b), structuring causes explain each and every tokening of the process they structure. In explaining why the dog salivates *when* the bell rings, I explain why it salivates *each* time the bell rings.

21. I hope it is clear that in speaking about organisms *becoming* conscious I am talking about types, not tokens. Natural selection does not make any particular giraffe's neck longer. It makes the necks of giraffes (the type) longer. Similarly, natural selection makes a type of organism conscious. It doesn't make any particular organism conscious.

22. Actually, some earlier token of this item type or, better, an earlier member of what Millikan (1984) calls the item's reproductive family.

23. An organ or trait can be selected without doing any useful job—this is what Lewontin and Gould (1979) call "a spandrel"—but it cannot be selected *for*—thus acquiring a function, something it is supposed to do—without doing useful work, without contributing in some way to reproductive success. For the distinction between selection *of* and selection *for*, see Sober 1984.

24. Ruth Millikan (1989a) has stressed the point that representations are dependent on *consumers*. I agree. If there is nothing to use (consume) the information provided, nothing can acquire the function of providing it. Nonetheless, the way information is consumed does not determine representational content. It does not tell us what the representation is a representation *of*. That is determined by *what* information the system acquires the function of providing.

25. It may have *become* useless, of course, because of an organism's changing needs, but it must once have been useful.

References

Akins, K. 1993. A bat without qualities. In Davies and Humphreys 1993, pp. 258–273.

Allport, A. 1988. What concept of consciousness? In Marcel and Bisiach 1988, pp. 159–182.

Armstrong, D. M. 1968. *A Materialist Theory of the Mind*. New York: Humanities Press.

Armstrong, D. M. 1980. *The Nature of Mind and Other Essays*. Ithaca, NY: Cornell University Press.

Armstrong, D. M. and N. Malcolm 1984. *Consciousness and Causality: A Debate on the Nature of Mind*. Oxford: Basil Blackwell.

Averbach, E., and Coriell, A. S. 1961. Short-term memory in vision. *Bell System Technical Journal*, 40: 309–328.

Baars, B. 1988. *A Cognitive Theory of Consciousness*. Cambridge: Cambridge University Press.

Bach, K. 1986. Thought and object: *de re* representations and relations. In Brand and Harnish 1986.

Bach, K. 1987. *Thought and Reference*. Oxford: Clarendon Press.

Baker, L. R. 1991. Dretske on the explanatory role of belief. *Philosophical Studies*, 63: 100–112.

Bennett, J. 1976. *Linguistic Behavior*. Cambridge, England: Cambridge University Press.

Bernecker, S. forthcoming. Propositional attitudes and self knowledge.

Bilgrami, A. 1992. Can externalism be reconciled with self-knowledge? *Philosophical Topics*, 20, no. 1: 233–267.

Biro, J. I. 1991. Consciousness and subjectivity.In Villanueva 1991, pp. 113–134.

Biro, J. I. 1993. Consciousness and objectivity. In Davies and Humphreys 1993a, pp. 178–196.

Bisiach, E. 1988. The haunted brain and consciousness. In Marcel and Bisiach 1988, pp. 101–120.

Bisiach, E. 1992. Understanding consciousness: clues from unilateral neglect and related disorders. In Milner and Rugg 1992, pp. 113–137.

Blakemore, C., and S. Greenfield, eds. 1987. *Mindwaves: Thoughts on Intelligence, Identity and Consciousness*. Oxford: Basil Blackwell.

Block, N., and J. Fodor 1972. What psychological states are not. *Philosophical Review*, 81: 159–181.

Block, N., ed. 1981. *Readings in the Philosophy of Psychology*. Cambridge, MA: Harvard.

Block, N. 1990a. Inverted Earth. In Tomberlin 1990, pp. 53–80.

Block, N. 1990b. Consciousness and accessibility. *Behavioral and Brain Sciences*, 13, no. 4: 596–598.

Block, N. 1991. Evidence against epiphenomenalism. *Behavioral and Brain Sciences*, 14, no. 4: 670–672.

Block, N. 1993. Review of Dan Dennett's *Consciousness Explained*. In *The Journal of Philosophy*.

Block, N., forthcoming. On a confusion about a function of consciousness. *Behavioral and Brain Sciences*.

Boghossian, P. 1989. Content and self knowledge. *Philosophical Topics*, 17, no. 1: 5–26.

Brentano, F. 1874. *Psychologie vom Empirischen Standpunkt*. Leipzig.

Brown, D. J. 1993. Swampman of La Mancha. *Canadian Journal of Philosophy* 23, no. 3: 327–348.

Burge, T. 1977. Belief *de re*. *Journal of Philosophy* 74: 338–362.

Burge, T. 1979. Individualism and the mental. *Midwest Studies in Philosophy IV: Studies in Metaphysics*, P. French et al., eds. Minneapolis: University of Minnesota Press.

Burge, T. 1982. Other bodies. *Thought and Object: Essays on Intentionality*, A. Woodfield, ed. Oxford: Clarendon Press.

Burge, T. 1988. Individualism and self knowledge. *Journal of Philosophy*, 85.

Carruthers, P. 1989. Brute experience. *Journal of Philosophy*, 86, no. 5: 258–269.

Carruthers, P. 1992. Consciousness and concepts II. *Aristotelian Society Proceedings*, pp. 41–59.

Cassam, Q., ed. 1994. *Self Knowledge*. Oxford: Oxford University Press.

Chisholm, R. 1957. *Perceiving: A Philosophical Study*. Ithaca, NY: Cornell University Press.

Christensen, C. B. 1993. Sense, subject and horizon. *Philosophy and Phenomenological Research*, 53, no. 4: 749–779.

Churchland, P. M. 1979. *Scientific Realism and the Plasticity of Mind*. Cambridge: Cambridge University Press.

Churchland, P. M. 1984. *Matter and Consciousness*; Cambridge, MA: MIT Press/A Bradford Book.

Churchland, P. M. 1989. *A Neurocomputational Perspective*. Cambridge, MA: MIT Press.

Churchland, P. S. 1988. Reduction and the neurobiological basis of consciousness. In Marcel and Bisiach 1988, pp. 273–304.

Clark, A. 1993a. *Sensory Qualities*. Oxford: Clarendon Press.

Clark, A. 1993b. Mice, shrews, and misrepresentation. *The Journal of Philosophy*, 90, no. 6: 290–310.

Cowey, A., and Petra Stoerig. 1992. Reflections on blindsight. In Milner and Rugg 1992, pp. 11–37.

Crane, T., ed. 1992a. *The Contents of Experience: Essays on Perception*; Cambridge: Cambridge University Press.

Crane, T. 1992b. Introduction. In Crane 1992, pp. 1–17.

Crane, T. 1993c. The nonconceptual content of experience. In Crane 1992a, pp. 136–157.

Cummins, R. 1975. Functional analysis. *Journal of Philosophy*, 72: 741–765.

Damasio, A. R., and H. Damasio 1993. Brain and language. In *Mind and Brain*. New York: W. H. Freeman and Co.

Davidson, D. 1984. First person authority. *Dialectica*, 38.

Davidson, D. 1987. Knowing one's own mind. *Proceedings and Addresses of the American Philosophical Association*, 60.

Davidson, D. 1988. Reply to Burge. *Journal of Philosophy*, 85: 664–665.

Davies, M. 1991. Individualism and perceptual content. *Mind*, 100, no. 4, Centennial Issue: 461–484.

Davies, M. 1992. Perceptual content and local supervenience. *Proceedings of the Aristotelian Society*, 92: 21–45.

Davies, M., and G. W. Humphreys, eds. 1993a. *Consciousness*. Oxford: Blackwell.

Davies, M., and G. W. Humphreys. 1993b. Introduction. In Davies and Humphreys 1993a, pp. 1–39.

Dennett, D. 1969. *Content and Consciousness*. London: Routledge and Kegan Paul.

Dennett, D. 1987. *The Intentional Stance*. Cambridge, MA: MIT Press.

Dennett, D. C. 1988. Quining qualia. In Marcel and Bisiach 1988, pp. 42–77.

Dennett, D. C. 1991a. *Consciousness Explained*. Little, Brown.

Dennett, D. C. 1991b. Postscript: Reflections: Instrumentalism reconsidered. In Rosenthal 1991.

Dennett, D. C. 1993. Living on the edge. *Inquiry*, 36, nos. 1 and 2: 135–160.

Dennett, D. C., and M. Kinsbourne. 1992. Time and the observer: The where and when of consciousness in the brain. *Behavioral and Brain Sciences*, 15, no. 2: 183–247.

Dretske, F. 1969. *Seeing and Knowing*. Chicago: University of Chicago Press.

Dretske, F. 1978. The role of the percept in visual cognition. In *Minnesota Studies in the Philosophy of Science: Perception and Cognition*, vol. 9, Wade Savage, ed. Minneapolis: University of Minnesota Press.

Dretske, F. 1979. Simple seeing. In *Body, Mind and Method: Essays in Honor of Virgil Aldrich*, D. F. Gustafson and B. L. Tapscott, eds. Dordrechet, Holland: Reidel.

Dretske, F. 1981. *Knowledge and the Flow of Information*. Cambridge, MA: MIT Press/A Bradford Book.

Dretske, F. 1986a. Misrepresentation. In *Belief*, Radu Bogdan, ed. Oxford: Oxford University Press.

Dretske, F. 1986b. Aspects of cognitive representation. In Brand and Harnish 1986.

Dretske, F. 1988. *Explaining Behavior*. Cambridge, MA: MIT Press.

Dretske, F. 1990a. Seeing, believing and knowing. In *An Invitation to Cognitive Science, Volume 2, Visual Cognition and Action*, D. Osherson, S. Kosslyn, and J. Hollerbach, eds. Cambridge, MA: MIT Press.

Dretske, F. 1990b. Does meaning matter? In *Information, Semantics and Epistemology*, Enrique Villanueva, ed. Oxford: Blackwell.

Dretske, F. 1991a. Dretske's replies. In McLaughlin 1991, 180–221.

Dretske, F. 1991b. How beliefs explain behavior: Reply to Baker. *Philosophical Studies*, 63: 113–117.

Dretske, F. 1992. What isn't wrong with folk psychology. *Metaphilosophy*, 23, nos. 1 and 2: 1–13.

Dretske, F. 1993a. Mental events as structuring causes of behavior. In Mele, A., and J. Heil eds., *Mental Causation*. Oxford: Oxford University Press, 121–136.

Dretske, F. 1993b. Can intelligence be artificial? *Philosophical Studies*, 71: 201–216.

Dretske, F. 1993c. Conscious experience. *Mind*, 102, no. 406: 263–283.

Dretske, F. 1994. Modes of perceptual representation. In *Philosophy and the Cognitive Sciences*, Roberto Casati, Barry Smith, and Graham White, eds. Vienna: Holder-Pichler-Tempsky.

Dretske, F., forthcoming. Differences that make no difference. *Philosophical Topics*.

Erdelyi, M. H. 1992. Psychodynamics and the unconscious. *American Psychologist*, 47, no. 6: 784–787.

Evans, G. 1982. *Varieties of Reference*. Oxford: Clarendon Press.

Ewert, J. P. 1987. Neuroethology of releasing mechanisms: prey-catching in toads. *Behavioral and Brain Sciences*, 10: 337–368.

Eysenck, M. W., ed. 1990. *The Blackwell Dictionary of Cognitive Psychology*. Oxford: Blackwell.

Favreau, O. E., and M. C. Corballis. 1976. Negative aftereffects in visual perception. Reprinted in Rock 1990, pp. 25–36.

Farah, M. J. 1990. *Visual Agnosia*. Cambridge, MA: MIT Press.

Fischbach, G. D. 1992. Mind and Brain. *Scientific American*, 267, no. 3: 48–57. Reprinted in *Mind and Brain*. New York: W. H. Freeman and Co., pp. 1–14.

Flanagan, O. 1992. *Consciousness Reconsidered*. Cambridge, MA: MIT Press.

Flavell, J. H. 1988. The development of children's knowledge about the mind: From cognitive connections to mental representations. In J. Astington, P. Harris, and D. Olson, eds., *Developing Theories of the Mind*. New York: Cambridge University Press.

Fodor, J. 1980. Methodological solipsism considered as a research strategy in cognitive psychology. In *The Behavioral and Brain Sciences*, 3.1: 63–72.

Fodor, J. 1983. *Modularity of Mind*. Cambridge, MA: MIT Press.

Fodor, J. 1987. *Psychosemantics*. Cambridge, MA: MIT Press.

Fodor, J. 1994. *Elm and The Expert: Mentalese and its Semantics*. Cambridge, MA: MIT Press.

Føllesdal, D. 1969. Husserl's notion of noema. *The Journal of Philosophy*, 66, no. 20: 680–687.

French, P. A., T. E. Uehling Jr., and H. K. Wettstein, eds. 1986. *Midwest Studies in Philosophy*. Vol. 10: *Studies in the Philosophy of Mind*. Minneapolis: University of Minnesota Press.

Gallistel, C. R. 1990. *The Organization of Learning*. Cambridge, MA: MIT Press.

Godfrey-Smith, P. 1989. Misinformation. *Canadian Journal of Philosophy*, 19, no. 4: 533–550.

Godfrey-Smith, P. 1994. A modern history theory of functions. *Nous*.

Goodman, N. 1976. *Languages of Art*. Indianapolis, IN: Hackett.

Gopnik, A. 1993. How do we know our minds: the illusion of first person knowledge of intentionality. *The Behavioral and Brain Sciences*, 16: 1–14.

Gould, S. J., and R. Lewontin. 1979. The sprandrels of San Marco and the Panglossian paradigm: A critique of the adaptationist programme. *Proceedings of the Royal Society* (London) B205: 581–598.

Grice, P. 1989. *Studies in the Way of Words*. Cambridge, MA: Harvard University Press.

Grier, J. W. 1984. *Biology of Animal Behavior*. St. Louis, MO: Times Mirror/Mosby.

Güzeldere, G. forthcoming. Is consciousness the perception of what passes in one's own mind? In *Towards a Scientific Basis for Consciousness*, S. Hameroff, A. Kasmiak, A. C. Scott, eds. Cambridge, MA: MIT Press.

Hall, G. 1981. Discrimination. In McFarland 1981.

Hardin, C. L. 1986. *Color for Philosophers*. Indianapolis, IN: Hackett.

Harman, G. 1990. The Intrinsic Quality of Experience. In Tomberlin 1990.

Hatfield, G. 1990. Gibsonian representations and connectionist symbol processing: prospects for unification. *Psychological Research*, 52: 243–252.

Hatfield, G. 1991. Representation in perception and cognition: connectionist affordances. *Philosophy and Connectionist Theory*, W. Ramsey, S. Stich, and D. Rumelhart, eds. Hillsdale, NJ: Lawrence Erlbaum.

Hatfield, G. 1992. Color perception and neural encoding: does metameric matching entail a loss of information. In M. Forbes and D. Hull, eds., *PSA 1992*, 2 volumes. East Lansing, MI: Philosophy of Science Association.

Hebb, D. O. 1969. The Mind's Eye. *Psychology Today*, 2, no. 12.

Heil, J. 1988. Privileged access. *Mind*, 47: 238–251.

Heil, J. 1992. *The Nature of True Minds*. Cambridge: Cambridge University Press.

Hilbert, D. R. 1987. *Color and Color Perception*. Stanford: Stanford University/CSLI.

Hilbert, D. R. 1992a. Comparative color vision and the objectivity of color. *Behavioral and Brain Sciences*, 15, no. 1: 38–39.

Hilbert, D. R. 1992b. What is color vision? *Philosophical Studies* 68: 351–370.

Horgan, T. 1984. Jackson on physical information and qualia. *Philosophical Quarterly*, 34: 147–151.

Horgan, T. 1991. Actions, reasons, and the explanatory role of content. In McLaughlin 1991, pp. 73–101.

Horgan, T., and J. Tienson, eds. 1991. *Connectionism and the Philosophy of Mind*. Dordrecht: Kluwer Academic Publishers.

Humphrey, N. 1970. What the frog's eye tells the monkey's brain. *Brain, Beh. Evol*, 3: 324–337.

Humphrey, N. 1972. Seeing and nothingness. *New Scientist*, 53: 682–684.

Humphrey, N. 1974. Vision in a monkey without striate cortex: a case study. *Perception*, 3: 241–255.

Humphrey, N. 1987. The inner eye of consciousness. In Blakemore and Greenfield 1987, pp. 377–382.

Humphrey, N. 1992. *A History of the Mind: Evolution and the Birth of Consciousness*. New York: Simon & Schuster.

Jackendoff, R. 1989. *Conscousness and the Computational Mind*. Cambridge, MA: MIT Press/A Bradford Book.

Jackson, F. 1977. *Perception*. Cambridge University Press.

Jackson, F. 1986. What Mary didn't know. *Journal of Philosophy*, 83: 291–295. Reprinted in Rosenthal 1991b, pp. 392–394.

Jacobs, G. H. 1981. *Comparative Color Vision*. New York: Academic Press.

Kanizsa, G. 1976. Subjective contours. Reprinted from *Scientific American* in *The Perceptual World*, I. Rock, ed. New York: W. H. Freeman and Co., pp. 155–163.

Kinsbourne, M. 1988. Integrated field theory of consciousness. In Marcel and Bisiach 1988, pp. 239–256.

Kitcher, P. 1993. Function and design. *Midwest Studies in Philosophy*, 18, *Philosophy of Science*, P. French, T. Uehling, Jr., and H. Wettstein, eds. Notre Dame, IN: University of Notre Dame Press, pp. 379–397.

Land, E. H. 1977. The retinex theory of color vision. *Scientific American*, 237, no. 6, 108–128.

Leeds, S. 1992. Qualia, awareness and Sellars. *Nous*.

LePore, E., and B. Loewer, 1986. Solipsistic Semantics. In French, et al. 1986, pp. 595–614.

Lettvin, J. Y., H. R. Maturana, W. S. McCulloch, and W. H. Pitts 1959. What the frog's eye tells the frog's brain. *Proceedings of the Institute of Radio Engineers*, 47: 1940–1951.

Lewicki, P., T. Hill, and M. Czyzewska 1992. Nonconscious acquisition of information. *American Psychologist*, 47, no. 6: 796–801.

Lewis, D. 1983. *Philosophical Papers*, volume 1. Oxford: Oxford University Press.

Lloyd, D. 1989. *Simple Minds*. Cambridge, MA: MIT Press.

Lloyd, D. 1991. Leaping to conclusions: connectionism, consciousness, and the computational mind. In Horgan and Tienson 1991, pp. 444–459.

Loar, B. 1990. Phenomenal states. In Tomberlin 1990, pp. 81–108.

Lycan, W. G. 1987. *Consciousness*. Cambridge, MA: MIT Press/A Bradford Book.

Lycan, W. G. 1990. What is the "Subjectivity" of the mental? In Tomberlin 1990.

Lyons, W. 1986. *The Disappearance of Introspection*. Cambridge, MA: MIT Press/A Bradford Book.

Marcel, A. J. 1988. Phenomenal experience and functionalism. In Marcel and Bisiach 1988, *Consciousness in Contemporary Science*. Oxford: Clarendon Press, pp. 121–158.

Marcel, A. J., and E. Bisiach. 1988. *Mental Representation and Consciousness*. Dordrecht: Kluwer.

Marr, D. 1982. *Vision*. San Francisco: W. H. Freeman and Co.

Matthen, M. 1988. Biological functions and perceptual content. *Journal of Philosophy*, 85, no. 1: 5–27.

McDowell, J. 1986. Singular thought and the extent of inner space. In P. Petit and J. McDowell, eds., *Subject, Thought and Context*. Oxford: Clarendon Press, pp. 137–168.

McFarland, D., ed. 1981. *The Oxford Companion to Animal Behavior*. Oxford: Oxford University Press.

McGinn, C. 1982. *The Character of Mind*. Oxford: Oxford University Press.

McGinn, C. 1989. *Mental Content*. Oxford: Blackwell.

McGinn, C. 1991. *The Problem of Consciousness*. Oxford: Blackwell.

McLaughlin, B. ed. 1991. *Critical Essays on the Philosophy of Fred Dretske*. Oxford: Blackwell.

Meltzoff, A. N., and Borton, R. W. 1979. Intermodal matching by human neonates. *Nature*, 282: 403–404.

Millar, A. 1991. *Reasons and Experience*. Oxford: Clarendon Press.

Miller, I. 1984. *Husserl*. Cambridge, MA: MIT Press.

Millikan, R. G. 1984. *Language, Thought, and Other Biological Categories: New Foundations for Realism*. Cambridge, MA: MIT Press.

Millikan, R. G. 1986. Thought without laws: cognitive science with content. *Philosophical Review*, 95.

Millikan, R. G. 1989a. Biosemantics. *Journal of Philosophy*, 86.

Millikan, R. G. 1989b. In defense of proper functions. *Philosophy of Science*, 56: 288–302.

Milner, A. D., and M. D. Rugg, eds. 1992. *The Neuropsychology of Consciousness*. London: Academic Press.

Milner, A. D. 1992. Disorders of perceptual awareness—commentary. In Milner and Rugg 1992, pp. 139–158.

Moore, G. E. 1922. The refutation of idealism. In *Philosophical Studies*. London: Routledge and Kegan Paul.

Nagel, T. 1974. What is it like to be a bat? *Philosophical Review*, 83, no. 4: 435–450.

Natsoulas, T. 1978. Consciousness. *American Psychologist*, 33: 906-14.

Natsoulas, T. 1983. Concepts of consciousness. *Journal of Mind and Behavior*, 4: 13–59.

Neander, K. 1991a. Functions as selected effects: the conceptual analyst's defence. *Philosophy of Science*, 58.

Neander, K. 1991b. The teleological notion of "function." *Australasian Journal of Philosophy*, 69.

Neisser, U. 1967. *Cognitive Psychology*. New York: Appleton-Century-Crofts.

Nemirow, L. 1980. Review of Nagel's *Mortal Questions*. *Philosophical Review* 89.

Nikolinakos, D. 1994. General anesthesia, consciousness, and the skeptical challenge. *Journal of Philosophy*, 91, no. 2: 88–104.

Noonan, H. W. 1993. Object-dependent thoughts: a case of superficial necessity but deep contingency? *Mental Causation*, J. Heil and A. Mele, eds. Oxford: Clarendon Press, pp. 283–308.

Paige, K. N., and T. G. Whitham. 1985. Report of research published in *Science*. *Scientific American*, 252, no. 4: 74.

Papineau, D. 1987. *Reality and Representation*. Oxford: Blackwell.

Papineau, D. 1993. *Philosophical Naturalism*. Oxford: Blackwell.

Peacocke, C. 1983. *Sense and Content*. Oxford: Clarendon Press.

Peacocke, C. 1992a. Scenarios, concepts and perception. In Crane 1992, pp. 105–135.

Peacocke, C. 1992b. *A Study of Concepts*. Cambridge, MA: MIT Press.

Penfield, W., and T. Rasmussen 1957. *A Clinical Study of Localization of Function*. New York: Macmillan.

Penfield, W., and L. Roberts 1959. *Speech and Brain Mechanisms*. Princeton, NJ: Princeton University Press.

Perkins, M. 1983. *Sensing the World*. Indianapolis, IN: Hackett Publishing Company.

Perner, J. 1991. *Understanding the Representational Mind*. Cambridge, MA: MIT Press.

Pitcher, G. 1971. *A Theory of Perception*. Princeton, NJ: Princeton University Press.

Pitcher, G. 1970. Pain perception. *Philosophical Review*, 79: 368–93.

Putnam, H. 1975. The meaning of "Meaning." *Language, Mind and Knowledge: Minnesota Studies in the Philosophy of Science*, vol. 7, K. Gunderson, ed. Minneapolis: University of Minnesota Press.

Pylyshyn, Z. W. 1978. When is attribtuion of beliefs justified? *The Behavioral and Brain Sciences*, 1: 592–593.

Quinton, A. 1977. In defense of introspection. *Philosophical Exchange*, 2: 77–88.

Recanati, F. 1993. *Direct Reference*. Oxford: Blackwell.

Reingold, E. M., and P. Merikle 1990. On the inter-relatedness of theory and measurement in the study of unconscious processes. *Mind and Language*, 5, no. 1: 9–28.

Rey, G. 1988. A question about consciousness. In H. Otto and J. Tuedio, eds., *Perspectives on Mind*. Dordrecht: Reidel.

Rey, G. 1992. Sensational sentences switched. *Philosophical Studies*, 68: 289–319.

Rey, G. 1993. Sensational sentences, in M. Davies and G. Humphyries, eds., *Consciousness*. Oxford: Blackwell.

Rosenthal, D. 1986. Two concepts of consciousness. *Philosophical Studies*, 94 no. 3: 329–359.

Rosenthal, D. 1990. A theory of consciousness. Report no. 40, Research Group on Mind and Brain, ZiF, University of Bielefeld.

Rosenthal, D. 1991a. The independence of consciousness and sensory quality. In Villanueva 1991, pp. 15–36.

Rosenthal, D. 1991b. *The Nature of Mind*. Oxford: Oxford University Press.

Rosenthal, D. 1993a. Higher-order thoughts and the appendage theory of consciousness. *Philosophical Psychology*, 6, no. 2: 155–166.

Rosenthal, D. 1993b. Multiple drafts and higher-order thoughts. *Philosophy and Phenomenological Research*, 53, no. 4: 911–918.

Rugg, M. D. 1992. Conscious and unconscious processes in language and memory—commentary. In Milner and Rugg 1992, pp. 263–278.

Seager, W. 1991. *Metaphysics of Consciousness*. London: Routledge.

Searle, J. 1992. *The Rediscovery of Mind*. Cambridge, MA: MIT Press.

Shapiro, L. 1993. Content, kinds, and individuation in Marr's theory of vision. *The Philosophical Review*, 102, no. 4: 489–513.

Shepard, R. N. 1992a. On the physical basis, linguistic representation, and conscious experience of colors. *Conception of the Mind: Essays in Honor of George A. Miller*, G. Harman, ed. Hillsdale, NJ: Lawrence Erlbaum Associates.

Shepard, R. N. 1992b. What in the world determines the structure of color space? *Behavioral and Brain Sciences*, 15, no. 1: 50–51.

Shoemaker, S. 1975. Functionalilsm and qualia. *Philosophical Studies*, 27: 292–315.

Shoemaker, S. 1986. Introspection and the self. From French, Uehling, and Wettstein 1986.

Shoemaker, S. 1990a. First-Person Access. In Tomberlin 1990.

Shoemaker, S. 1990b. Qualities and Qualia: What's in the mind. *Philosophy and Phenomenological Research*, 50, Supplement: 109–131.

Shoemaker, S. 1991. Qualia and consciousness. *Mind*, 100, no 4, Centennial Issue: 507–524.

Shoemaker, S. 1993a. Lovely and suspect ideas. *Philosophy and Phenomenological Research*, 53, no. 4: 905–910.

Shoemaker, S. 1993b. Special access lies down with theory-theory. *Behavioral and Brain Sciences*, 16, no. 1: 78–79.

Shoemaker, S 1994. Self knowledge and "Inner Sense," The Royce Lectures. *Philosophy and Phenomenological Research*, 54, no. 2: 249–314.

Sober, E. 1984. *The Nature of Selection*. Cambridge, MA: MIT Press.

Sperling, G. 1960. The information available in brief visual presentations. *Psychological Monographs*, 74, no. 11.

Stalnaker, R. 1990. Narrow content. *Propositional Attitudes*, ed. C. A. Anderson and J. Owens. Stanford: CSLI, 249–314.

Stampe, D. 1977. Towards a causal theory of linguistic representation. In P. French, T. Uehling and H. Wettstein, eds., *Midwest Studies in Philosophy*, vol. 2, *Studies in Semantics*. Minneapolis: University of Minnesota Press.

Stein, B. E., and M. A. Meredith 1993. *The Merging of the Senses*. Cambridge, MA: MIT Press.

Sterelny, K. 1990. *The Representational Theory of the Mind*. Oxford: Blackwell.

Stich, S. 1983. *From Folk Psychology to Cognitive Science: The Case Against Belief*. Cambridge: MIT Press.

Stoerig, P. and A. Cowey 1992. Wavelength processing and colour experience. *Behavioral and Brain Sciences*, 15, no.1: 53.

Tomberlin, J. E. 1990. *Philosophical Perspectives, 4: Action Theory and Philosophy of Mind*, Atascadero, CA: Ridgeview.

Treisman, M. 1992. Does the perception of temporal sequence throw light on consciousness. *Behavioral and Brain Sciences*, 15, no .2: 225–228.

Tye, M. 1986. The subjective qualities of experience. *Mind*, 95: 1–17.

Tye, M. 1989. *The Metaphysics of Mind*. Cambridge, England: Cambridge University Press.

Tye, M. 1991. *The Imagery Debate*. Cambridge, MA: MIT Press.

Tye, M. 1992. Visual qualia and visual content. In Crane 1992, pp. 158–176.

Tye, M. 1994. Qualia, content, and the inverted spectrum. *Nous*.

Umilt, C. 1988. The control operations of consciousness. In Marcel and Bisiach 1988, pp. 334–356.

Valberg, J. J. 1992. *The Puzzle of Experience*. Oxford: Clarendon Press.

Van der Heijden, A. H. C. 1992. *Selective Attention in Vision*. London: Routledge.

van Gulick, R. 1989. What difference does consciousness make? *Philosophical Topics*, 17: 211–230.

van Gulick, R. 1993. Understanding the phenomenal mind: are we all just armadillos? In Davies and Humphries 1993, pp. 137–154.

Velmans, M. 1991. Is human information processing conscious? *Behavioral and Brain Sciences*, 14, no. 4: 651–668.

Villanueva, E., ed. 1991. *Consciousness*. Atascadero, CA: Ridgeview.

Walker, S. 1983. *Animal Thought*. London: Routledge and Kegan Paul.

Weiskrantz, L. 1988a. Some contributions of neuropsychology of vision and memory to the problem of consciousness. In Marcel and Bisiach 1988, pp. 183–199.

Weiskrantz, L., ed. 1988b. *Thought without Language*. Oxford: Clarendon Press.

Weiskrantz, L. 1991. Introduction: Dissociated Issues. In Milner and Rugg 1991, pp. 1–10.

Wellman, H. M. 1990. *The Child's Theory of the Mind*. Cambridge, MA: MIT Press/A Bradford Book.

White, A. R. 1964. *Attention*. Oxford: Basil Blackwell.

Wilkes, K. V. 1988. ——, yishi, duh, um and consiousness. *Consciousness in Contemporary Science*, A. J. Marcel and E. Bisiach, eds. Oxford: Clarendon Press.

Wittgenstein, L. 1974. *Philosophical Investigations*. Oxford: Basil Blackwell.

Wright, C. 1991. Wittgenstein's later philosophy of mind: sensation, privacy and intention. *Meaning Scepticism*, K. Puhl, ed. Berlin: de Gruyter, pp. 126–147.

Wright, L. 1973. Functions. *Philosophical Review*, 82: 139–168.

Wright, L. 1976. *Teleological Explanations*. Berkeley: University of California Press.

Young, A. W., and E. H. F. de Haan 1990. Impairments of visual awareness. *Mind and Language*, 5, no. 1: 29–48.

Young, A. W., and E. H. F. de Haan 1992. Face recognition and awareness after brain injury. In Milner and Rugg 1992, pp. 69–90.

Zeki, S. 1992. The visual image in mind and brain. *Scientific American*, 267, no. 3: 69–76. Reprinted in *Mind and Brain*. New York: W. H. Freeman and Co., pp. 27–39.

Index